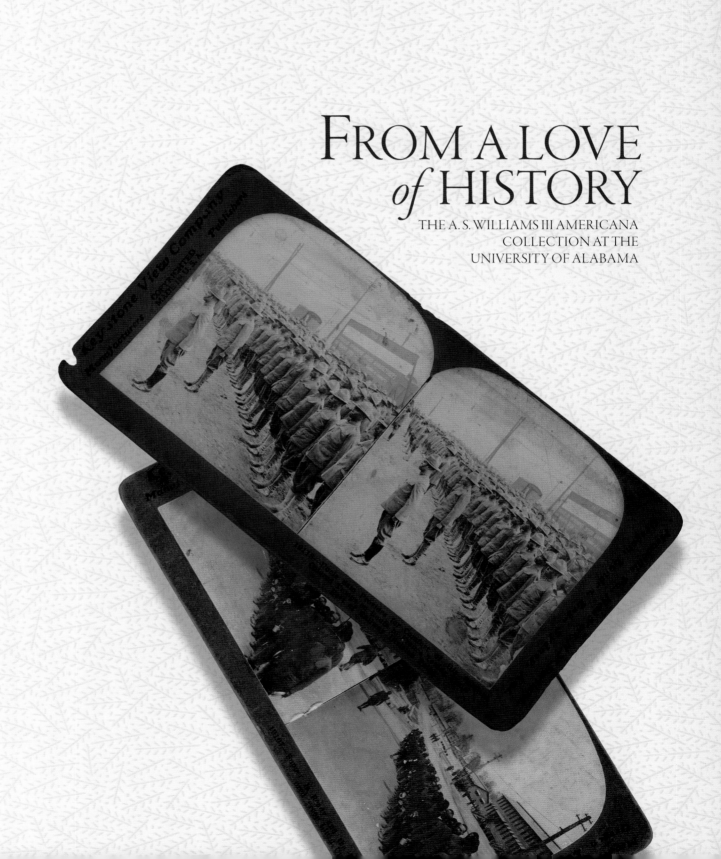

FROM A LOVE
of HISTORY

THE A. S. WILLIAMS III AMERICANA
COLLECTION AT THE
UNIVERSITY OF ALABAMA

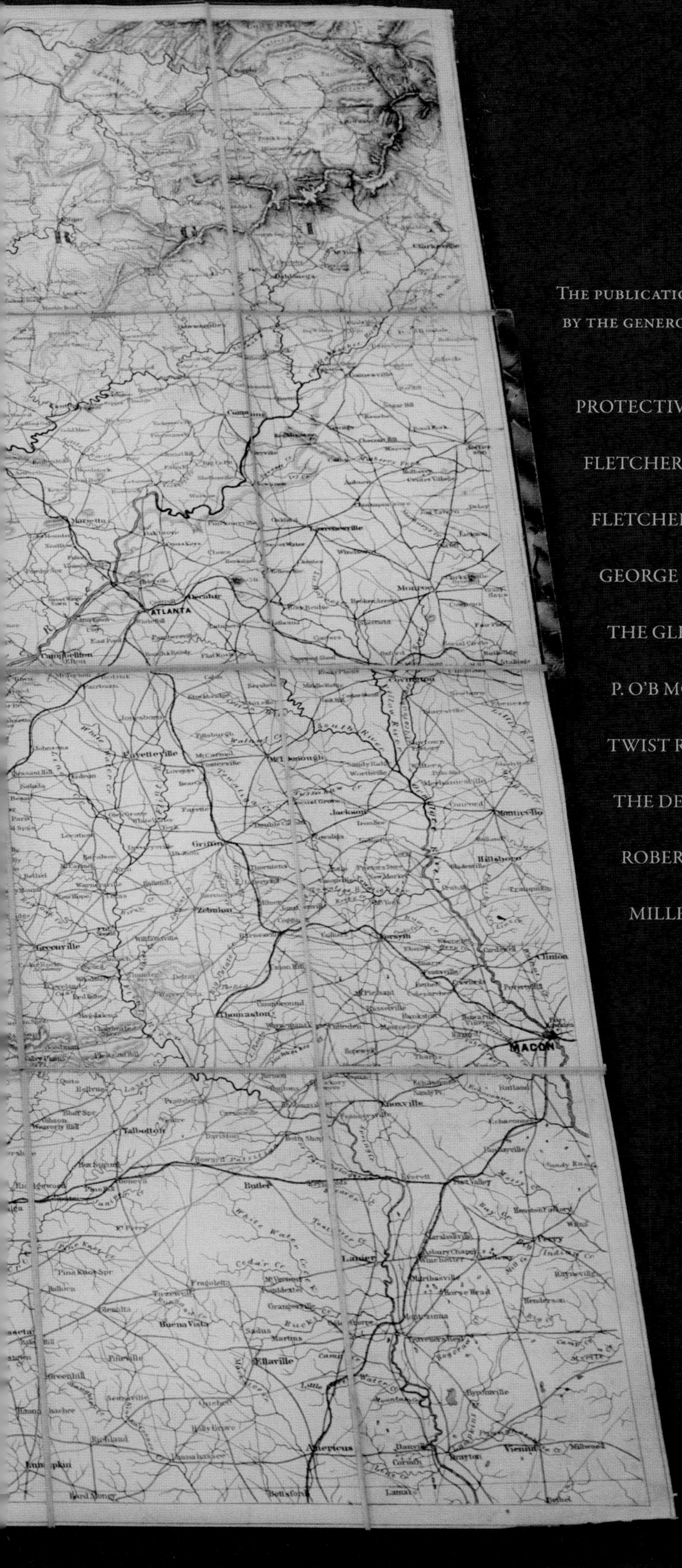

The publication of this volume was made possible
by the generous support of the following:

PROTECTIVE LIFE CORPORATION

FLETCHER BRIGHT COMPANY

FLETCHER BRIGHT COMPANY—ATLANTA

GEORGE B. HUBER

THE GLENWOOD DEVELOPMENT COMPANY, LLC

P. O'B MONTGOMERY & CO.

TWIST REALTY LP

THE DEWBERRY FOUNDATION, INC.

ROBERT K. CARLIN

MILLER & MARTIN PLLC

True Rose.

Just when the red June Rose ...
She gave me one — a year ago ...
A Rose whose crimson breath ...
The scent that its heart ...
And — half shy, half true ...
Blushing, stood upon the gir...
Just as ... — a year as ...

... as not to ...
... I plucked her ...
It — half th...
I laid it ...
The calm ...
And ...

... each other
... ts are faithful
... will not see
... ing breath.
... my darling, seals,
... death !
            Rarie Holm.

... tenderer, — as if a new life had
... that extraordinates the old — as
... one had set, the new had
            Stay of Seventahs.

... congenial mate for a woman of sentiment
... well-educated German : for such a
... strong sense of family ties, a
... disposition toward the predic...
            The Parisians ...

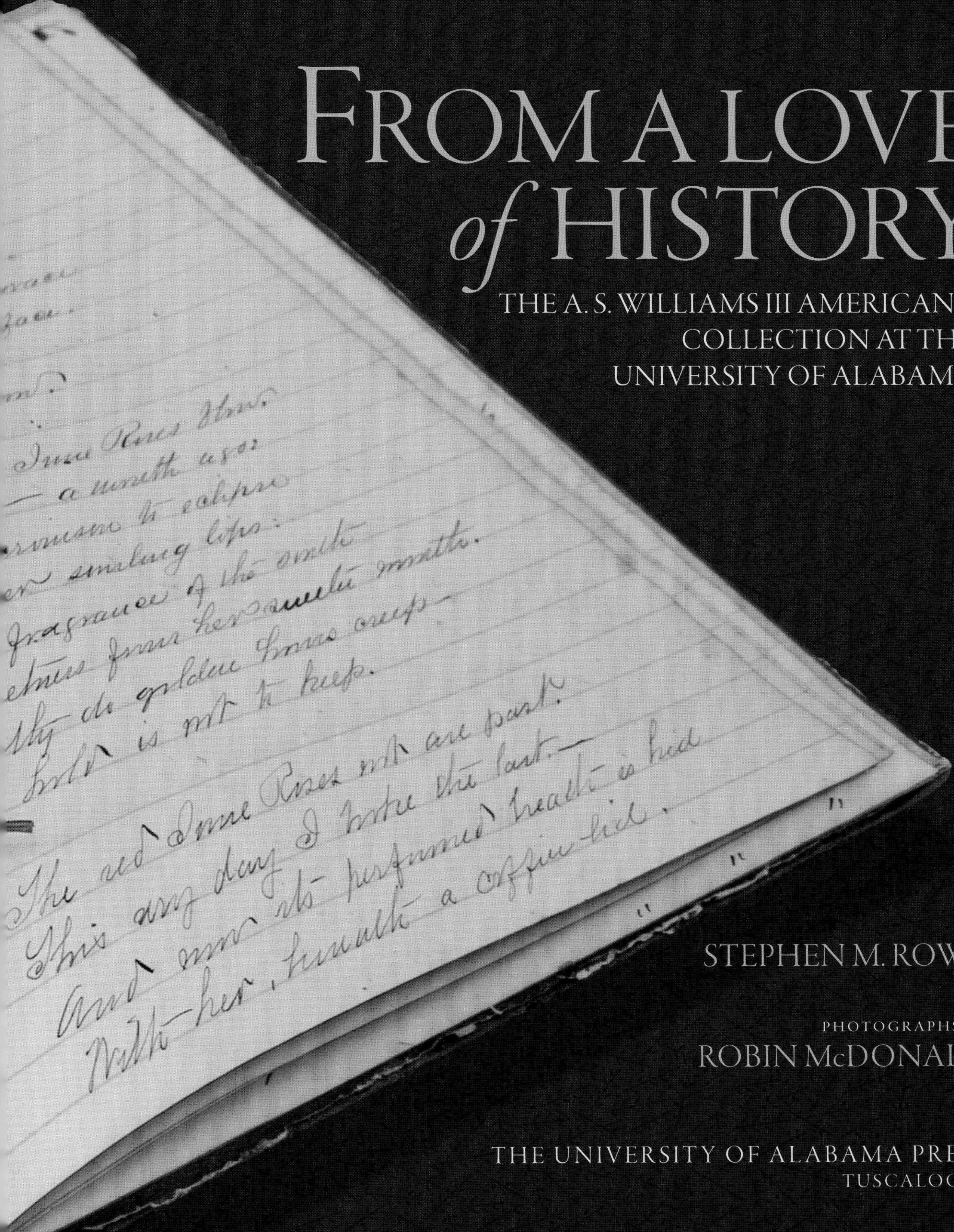

FROM A LOVE of HISTORY

THE A. S. WILLIAMS III AMERICANA COLLECTION AT THE UNIVERSITY OF ALABAMA

STEPHEN M. ROWE

PHOTOGRAPHS BY
ROBIN McDONALD

THE UNIVERSITY OF ALABAMA PRESS
TUSCALOOSA

PUBLISHED IN COOPERATION WITH
THE UNIVERSITY LIBRARIES, THE UNIVERSITY OF ALABAMA

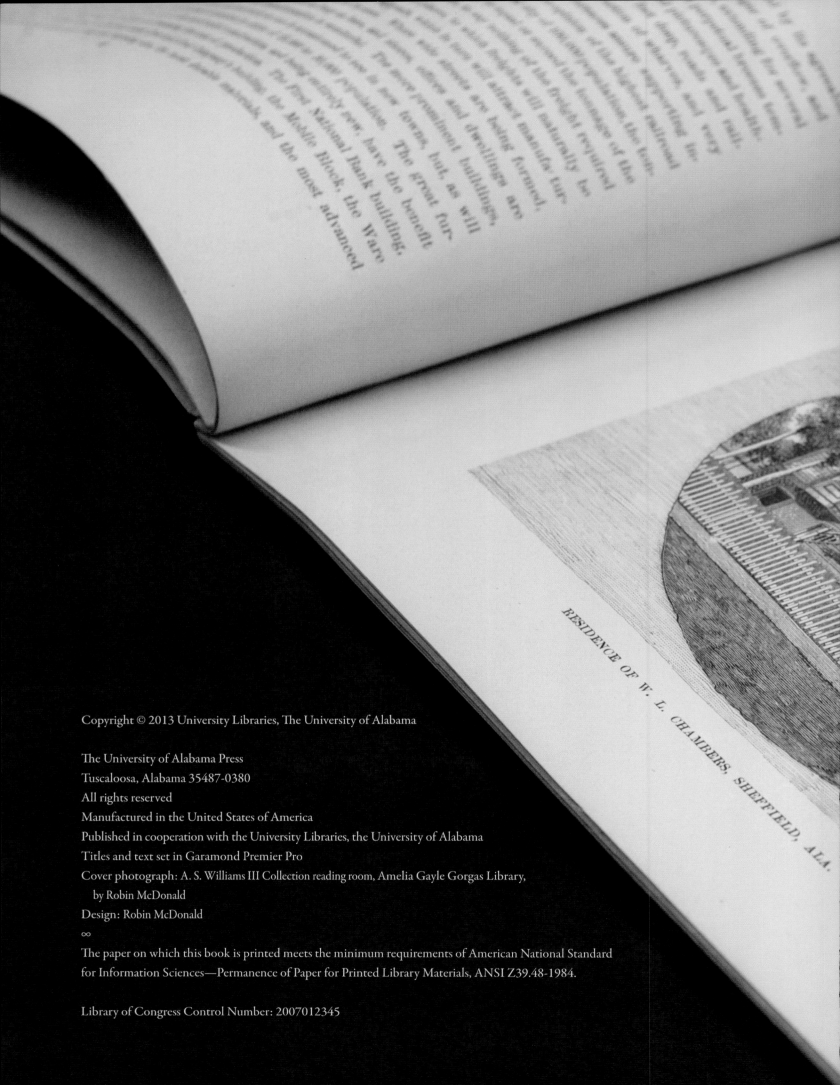

The University of Alabama Press
Tuscaloosa, Alabama 35487-0380
All rights reserved
Manufactured in the United States of America
Published in cooperation with the University Libraries, the University of Alabama
Titles and text set in Garamond Premier Pro
Cover photograph: A. S. Williams III Collection reading room, Amelia Gayle Gorgas Library,
   by Robin McDonald
Design: Robin McDonald
∞
The paper on which this book is printed meets the minimum requirements of American National Standard
for Information Sciences—Permanence of Paper for Printed Library Materials, ANSI Z39.48-1984.

Library of Congress Control Number: 2007012345

CONTENTS

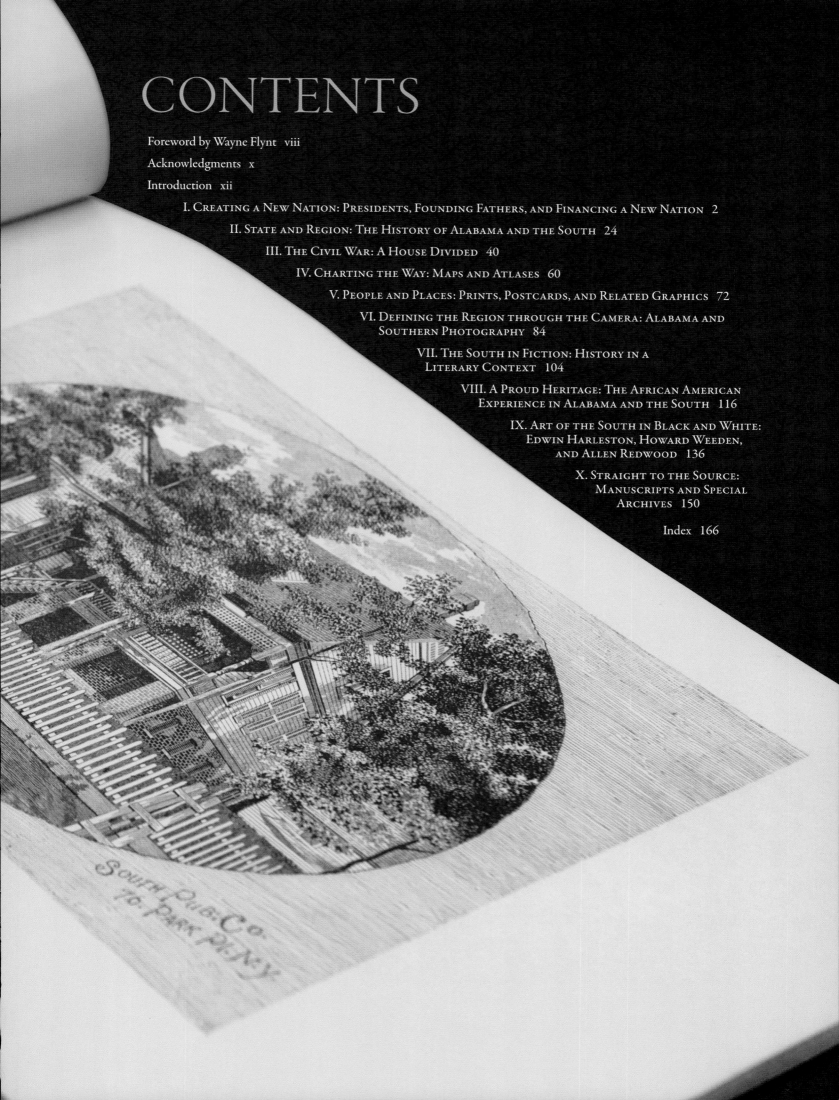

FOREWORD

WHILE SPENDING MANY wonderful hours exploring the A. S. Williams III Americana Collection of Alabama/American history, art, literature, and politics at the Eufaula Athenaeum, I concluded that this was an Alabama treasure pretty much beyond price. The treasures it contains are often one of a kind. It includes extremely rare photos of African American life in Tuskegee, books and photographs so uncommon that only a handful (or, in some cases, only a single copy) exist, artists' impressions of a disappearing landscape, and supplemental historical records.

Because I am quintessentially a book person, I relished holding in my hands a first edition of Harper Lee's magical novel *To Kill a Mockingbird*, perhaps the most beloved American novel of the twentieth century and now the most iconic and unifying cultural fragment of Alabama in the 1930s in terms of recognition and familiarity. If one single piece of literature stirs universal recognition in Americans living today, beyond the Bible at least, it is Lee's eternally relevant coming-of-age story of how one generation passes to another its most sacred and enduring moral and ethical values: tolerance, kindness, generosity even to those whom we do not understand, integrity, moral courage, and independence of community and peer values that diminish our own. In these contentious times, when I held that first edition in my hands, I rejoiced that it was an Alabama novelist from the edge of the Black Belt who taught Americans most simply and directly what is best about us as a people. And, of course, first editions of the books written by her Monroeville best friend, Truman Capote, in alternating anguished (*Other Voices, Other Rooms*) and lilting (*The Grass Harp* and *A Christmas Memory*) prose, invited me to enter another world of tolerance and joyous remembrance.

I have long been fascinated by the intellectual history of book collecting and book collectors. Being one myself on a small scale, I was fascinated by the eclecticism of the A. S. Williams Collection. Holdings ran from obsession to obsession: political history of every president and administration in American history, priceless regimental histories of a remarkable range of Civil War military units

(particularly Confederate and Alabama ones), an encyclopedic collection of Tuskegee photographs, and a virtual literary Fort Knox of invaluable first editions by southern authors. Indeed, the strength of the collection is its eclecticism and depth within each collectable category of interest.

I have read many wonderful books about the adventure of book collecting—Helene Hanff's *84, Charing Cross Road*; Lawrence and Nancy Goldstone's *Used and Rare: Travels in the Book World*; Harold Rabinowitz and Rob Kaplan's *A Passion For Books: A Book Lover's Treasury of Stories, Essays, Humor, Lore, and Lists on Collecting, Reading, Borrowing, Lending, Caring for, and Appreciating Books*; Frye Gaillard, *The Books That Mattered: A Reader's Memoir*—all of which explore not only books, but the mind of a fanatical collector/reader. Steve Williams fits that intellectual addiction, a man who wanted to know all there was to know about everything pertaining to Alabama and to preserve records, art, photographs, pamphlets, books, and other materials too priceless and rare to be lost. Were we to lose those, he reasoned, we would lose a part of ourselves.

This book will take its place with the others I love, telling the story of a journey of discovery and describing what was found. It is unique in its obsession with topics (early American political and national history), a region of the country (the South, black and white, centered in the Civil War, the region's most important event), and a state (everything pertaining to Alabama). This book, skillfully shaped around these themes, becomes a window not only into the mind of a curious collector, but also into a monumental collection, itself a primary document in the history of a people. And the artifacts themselves described in this book will tease, seduce, tempt, and finally obsess others as it did the collection's founder and me.

Wayne Flynt,
Distinguished University Professor Emeritus,
Auburn University

ACKNOWLEDGMENTS

M
Y NEARLY THIRTY-
year association with Steve Williams has been one of the greatest
privileges of my career as an antiquarian bookseller. As my client
and my friend, Steve honored me with his request that I come to
Eufaula, Alabama, and assume curatorial and collection development
duties for the Eufaula Athenaeum. I was further privileged by the
request of the University of Alabama Libraries, through Dean Louis
Pitschmann, that I author this book. His confidence and support have
been greatly appreciated.

I would like to thank Nancy Dupree and the staff of the A. S.
Williams III Americana Collection at the University of Alabama
Libraries for assisting me in a most gracious and efficient manner. I am
indeed fortunate that Robin McDonald, an outstanding photographer and a man of rare humor, was selected to produce the illustrations
and design the book. My conversion from a typewriter to a computer
for this project was made tolerable through the efforts of my
associate Phillip Mars. Finally, my thanks to the staff of
the University of Alabama Press for their cordial
assistance in publishing the story of Steve
Williams's remarkable collection.

TITLE PAGE AND FRONT COVER OF PAUL LAURENCE
DUNBAR'S *POEMS OF CABIN AND FIELD* (1904).

Paul Laurence Dunbar (1872–1906) was the son of former
slaves and the first African American poet to receive national
acclaim. An early interest in poetry, nurtured by his
mother, led to the publication of his first book
of poems in 1892. Dunbar wrote both
dialect and standard English poems
with equal facility. His literary output included not only poetry, but
also essays, short stories, and novels.
His brilliant career was cut short by his
death at thirty-three.

IMAGE CAPTIONS

PAGE I: Two stereoviews of African American troops training for
World War I; PAGES II–III: Folding map of northern Alabama and
Georgia, issued to federal forces in the field during the Civil War;
PAGES IV–V: Journal, with dried flowers, kept by noted Alabama artist
Howard Weeden; PAGE VI–VII: Spread from a Sheffield promotional
brochure showing the residence of W. L. Chambers; PAGE VIII: Front
cover of Harper Lee's *To Kill a Mockingbird*; PAGE IX: Access to the
stacks of the Williams Collection is restricted to staff only. PAGES
XVI–1: A July 31, 1864, affidavit supporting a petition by Mrs. Sarah
Lavender of Pickens County, Alabama, to have her husband, James J.
Lavender, a private in the Second Alabama Cavalry, discharged from
the Confederate army.

INTRODUCTION

WITH OVER FORTY YEARS of collecting behind him, A. S. (Steve) Williams III had to finally face the fact that his collection of books, manuscripts, photographs, maps, prints, and paintings had outgrown his Birmingham home. His books on US presidents were already lodged in rented office space, and some books were without shelf space in the house. Williams initially thought to keep his collection in his adopted city of Birmingham, Alabama. Upon further reflection he decided to move it to his hometown of Eufaula, in Barbour County, Alabama, a place his family has lived for many generations. The idea for what became the Eufaula Athenaeum was conceived, and the collection's first odyssey was about to begin.

An antebellum building in the downtown business district was available and purchased by Williams in 2000. A local architect and a local contractor transformed the 6,500-square-foot building, lining the walls and alcoves with bookcases, which would eventually hold over twenty-two thousand volumes. Display cases and a fire-resistant walk-in vault, replete with fire-resistant filing cabinets and a fire-resistant safe, completed the necessary requirements for housing the collection. That, in retrospect, may have been the easy part.

Next some twenty thousand volumes, an almost overflowing ten-drawer map and print case, boxes containing perhaps as many as ten thousand photographs, and numerous artifacts and original works of art had to be moved. With some minor exceptions, Williams and a single assistant packed and unpacked every item. By the spring of 2005 the required multiple moves were completed. The Eufaula Athenaeum was ready to become part of the deep roots that connect Steve Williams to this historic locale of Alabama history.

Williams's book collecting had begun with his return to Eufaula after his graduation from the University of Alabama in 1958. The collection was primarily devoted to American history, with some titles having been found in old homes around the city. After working in Eufaula for a year, Williams and his wife, Rosemary Hoover Williams, also a 1958 graduate of the university, decided to move to Birmingham. The books did not accompany the Williamses initially, and when Williams inquired about them later, he discovered they had been given away.

When queried about any early interest in history, Williams replied, "The only D I ever got in school was in fourth grade Alabama history." This did not result from any disinterest, according to Williams, but

ABOVE: *A. S. (Steve) Williams III.* FACING PAGE: *In 2005, Williams relocated his collection to an elegantly refurbished storefront on the main street of his hometown of Eufaula.*

was a reflection of his somewhat chaotic school days and family life during World War II. Later, at the University of Alabama he took the standard Western civilization class and one in foreign history but none in American history. His focus was on his classes in his major studies, business and finance.

Williams's first job in Birmingham was with First National Bank, and in the early 1960s the bank sent him to a conference in Virginia. Free time allowed for a day trip to Williamsburg, the restored capital of colonial Virginia. He purchased a few books on early American history on that trip, which was the first of several visits.

The genesis of the extensive collection Williams ultimately built on the American presidency began with this sojourn in Williamsburg. The trip rekindled the interest in American history he remembers having in some form since childhood. Williams began his presidential collection with the earliest presidents but soon moved into a more comprehensive mode, deciding that a history of these men and their administrations is, in the main, a history of the country.

Thomas Jefferson was Williams's initial favorite among presidents, with Washington a close second. Jefferson's appeal was, according to Williams, in "his multiplicity of talents, his intellectual accomplishments. In a number of ways Jefferson was head and shoulders above many of his fellow founders in intellect. He was a patriot, and I found him to be the most fascinating president in my early collection." Williams found Washington to be "the most selfless of the founding fathers," stating, "I believe he was a true patriot who placed the good of the country above his own personal agenda. He had all the right motives for putting the country on a sound footing, without doubt the right man to be our first president."

Williams's interest in the evolution of the founding principles of the country led him to an admiration for James Madison and Alexander Hamilton. Williams's career in the financial sector as a senior officer at the Protective Life Insurance Company gave him an appreciation for Hamilton's business acumen: "His considerable responsibility, along with Robert Morris, in placing the United States on a sound financial footing was a major accomplishment. It makes one wonder what more he would have accomplished in government and the private sector had he not been killed in the duel with Burr."

Patrick Henry and John Adams are two other founders for whom Williams has high regard: "John Adams, in my opinion, was remarkable in his consistent purpose to 'do the right thing' as he saw it,

regardless of personal or political consequences. That seems to be the overriding theme of his life and undoubtedly limited him to a single term as president."

Other figures from the early history of the nation, such as Aaron Burr and James Wilkinson, hold Williams's interest as well. Williams considers Burr "a man of great talent, highly intelligent, whose schemes, while proving beneficial to Burr and his associates, indicate a lack of integrity." The A. S. Williams III Americana Collection contains a number of volumes on Burr, the conspiracy, and General Wilkinson's involvement therein.

The collection of presidential documents in the Williams Collection derives from Steve Williams's desire to "touch" history. Holding a document once held and signed by a president or any other historical figure "creates a unique feeling" for him, a connection perhaps hard to explain but appreciated by any collector of manuscripts. The collection contains at least one document signed by every president through George W. Bush.

From this substantial beginning Williams began to branch out, initially collecting significant books on Alabama history. This eventually led to the formation of one of the most important personal libraries in the state. In addition to rare books, such as Thomas Woodward's reminiscences and the writings of important regional travelers like William Bartram, Williams acquired important ancillary groups, including an archive of early Alabama almanacs and a major collection of promotional literature related to cities, towns, and other localities

in the state. According to Williams, the decision to expand the collection into one of regional history was never a conscious one, "it just happened." In addition to a number of rare and important titles, the Williams Collection is rich in eighteenth- and nineteenth-century southern travel accounts.

Alabama's prominent role in the Civil War led to an interest in the entire history of the conflict, from both the Southern and Northern perspectives. While the military aspects of the war are best represented in the collection, the economic, social, and political facets receive thorough treatment. Williams began this segment of the collection from a general personal interest and was hesitant to commit to a comprehensive effort because of the vast number of books and pamphlets on the subject. Once he decided to build the collection in this area it "eventually became the controlling factor," he recalled. "I extended myself more in that area than in any other." His commitment to that is amply demonstrated by his acquisition of a set of *Gardner's Photographic Sketch Book of the War*, the most important volume of Civil War photography (Union general Philip Henry Sheridan's set, no less), as well as his assembling one of the most important groups of Confederate imprints in private hands. With the acquisition of the Williams Collection the University of Alabama moved into an elite group, with forty-five unique imprints in an archive of over five hundred. The photographic and cartographic archive of Union topographical engineer Captain William Margedant, an important collection of imprints related to the Neale Publishing Company, and a copy of William W. Heartsill's extremely rare hand-printed Confederate memoir, *Fourteen Hundred and 91 Days in the Confederate Army*, define the intense passion with which Williams pursued his interest.

"At first I resisted the concept of collecting maps, but my overriding interest in Alabama history started me in that direction," says Williams. "From there, like the other portions of the collection, it just grew." In addition to a number of early and important maps related to the state, the map archive contains a number of rare Civil War maps, including a small group printed in the Confederacy. The collection also contains a set of the *Official Atlas to Accompany the War of the Rebellion* and a number of early maps of the southeast United States. The business of insurance is represented by a substantial collection of Alabama-related insurance maps.

The Williams postcard collection is primarily related to Confederate themes and regional history. The prints and lithographs cover the

Williams enjoys a moment of contemplation at his desk in the Eufaula Athenaeum (Photograph by Carla Caforio).

same general areas with the addition of numerous historical personages of national significance. Some items, the print of Creek Native American Paddy Carr, for example, came from a grouping formed by an earlier Alabama collector, in the Carr case Peter A. Brannon. According to Williams the prints and postcards "were just a logical progression."

Photography began to capture Williams's interest in the mid-1970s. His initial purchases were almost exclusively related to Alabama. Family albums and photographic groupings related to families are of special significance to Williams, and he will admit he has "bought these indiscriminately." Civil War photography soon followed, to provide a visual accompaniment to the already burgeoning book collection. The crowning piece in this portion of the collection is the previously mentioned copy of *Gardner's Photographic Sketch Book of the War*. This extremely rare set, of which fewer than twenty exist in complete form, is supplemented by numerous war-date stereoviews and cartes de visite. Battlefield scenes and important personages from both North and South as well as war-time general views of places associated with the conflict comprise a significant archive. The Williams Collection has extensive holdings in images related to documenting the work places and work periods of southern photographers active throughout the region, covering primarily the period from 1860 to 1910.

The southern fiction collection was begun in the mid-1990s. Williams already had a few important and collectable titles and had always been interested in how the South was portrayed in fiction.

He was especially interested in the Vanderbilt group of prose and poetry writers, and both the Fugitive and Agrarian movements are well represented in the collection. Williams had read portions of *I'll Take My Stand* and some related writings and was taken by how these authors "wrote Southern history and addressed enduring Southern themes and values through fiction."

Among modern southern authors, Williams has an affinity for John Grisham: "I like novels based on legal issues and the art of detection. Part of this, I suppose, comes from my own legal background. [Williams is a graduate of the Birmingham School of Law but did not practice the profession.] I thought *A Time to Kill* was one of the best books I have ever read. John Grisham is an excellent storyteller and holds a reader's interest. I've read virtually all of his books." The Williams Collection contains first editions of every one of Grisham's books published prior to 2010, and a number of limited signed editions.

With his abiding interest in all things related to his state, Williams has assembled a most impressive collection relating to the African American experience in Alabama. Books written by Booker T. Washington were early additions to the library and Williams read deeply in *The Future of the American Negro*. Interest in Washington led to an interest in the Tuskegee Institute as well as black schools and colleges throughout the state. The collection has several archives related to Tuskegee, one from an early music teacher and choir director Jennie C. Lee. Another is from alumnus Ephraim M. Henry who sang in the choir and received a degree in science. Several photographic albums related to the Lincoln Normal School in Marion provide a unique documentary insight into that famous institution in the 1920s. Williams recalls being shown the Lee archive by a Nashville book dealer. "It was in a grocery bag, in terrible disorder and generally poor condition. But I realized its significance and was determined to see that it survived as intact as possible."

The most important group of original art in the Williams Collection is a series of canvasses by noted African American artist Edwin Augustus Harleston. The Charleston native and civil rights activist did primarily portraiture and landscapes but assisted Aaron Douglas with the renowned murals at Fisk University. The paintings in the Williams Collection are mainly portraits but include a self-portrait in charcoal and some anatomical drawings. The Harleston paintings were acquired as a group from a former instructor at Miles College in Birmingham. The collection also holds a large watercolor by Alabama artist Maria Howard Weeden. Some of Weeden's notebooks in the manuscript collection contain pen and ink sketches related to her interest in Washington Irving's "The Legend of Sleepy Hollow."

The manuscript collection is, as may be expected, extremely diverse. Union and Confederate diaries and letters, unpublished book manuscripts relating to the history of various localities in the state, and documented photographic albums form just a portion of the collection. Williams was especially interested in groups related to Alabama families as well as institutional and business records. A prime example of the latter is the 1863 guest register for the famed Battle House hotel in Mobile. When queried about the breadth and depth of the manuscript collection, Williams says, "I went about collecting these things in my own way, always with an eye for each item's historical significance."

Indeed, the same thing could be said about the entire collection. Williams will admit that he could have created "a more meaningful collection had I taken a more narrow focus. But such recognition as the collection may receive should result from the final accomplishment, not the methodology."

There are some parallels between Steve Williams and one of his favorite founding fathers, Thomas Jefferson. Jefferson once wrote to John Adams, "I cannot live without books." This was in June 1815 and was occasioned by the acquisition of his library by Congress as a replacement for the loss of the congressional library at the hands of the British in 1814. That collection, nearly 6,500 volumes, had been carefully assembled by Jefferson and was considered by some, including Jefferson himself, to be the finest private library in the United States. Yet the separation of a true collector and his books is never an easy process. Though Jefferson did benefit financially from the transaction, he believed that his books could serve the greater good by providing the members of our governing body with the knowledge they contained. Jefferson, following his lament to Adams, immediately began a second collection.

Steve Williams's goal as a collector was never centered on keeping the collection simply for his own gratification. The choice of the term *athenaeum*, adopted from a visit to the Boston Athenaeum, is indicative of this. He defined the Eufaula Athenaeum not in the classical sense, per se, but as an institution devoted to collecting and preserving material relating to the history and culture of the American republic, especially the southern states of that republic and most specifically the state of Alabama.

No requests for assistance or use by scholars was ever refused, save on grounds of unavailability of sources. Materials have been graciously loaned to other museums to enhance exhibitions and promote scholarly pursuits. Visiting scholars, archivists, and lovers of history began to spread the word of this remarkable collection, its scope, and the character of its owner. It remained, however, for the University of Alabama, through its dean of libraries, Louis Pitschmann, to embrace the concept that this unique collection should remain intact and in the state of Alabama. It was Williams's desire that it be kept together and Dean Pitschmann heartily concurred. Negotiations for its acquisition by the University of Alabama Libraries culminated in the summer of 2010, and the collection became a separate entity of the Amelia Gayle Gorgas Library, with a dedicated space and curator.

With his legacy assured, A. S. Williams, like Thomas Jefferson, remained true to his collector self and began collecting anew.

The State of Alabama }
Pickens County } To all before whom these presents
may come Sarah A Launder
Wife of James I Launder
The undersigned Sarah A Launder
Wife of James I Launder who is a private of Compan[y]
C. 2[n]d Alabama Cavalry would respectfully repre-
sent under oath the following statement of facts;

That her said husband Jas I is an unsound
man in body, and has been diseased for a number
of years; that he has not been able to do any duty
since he has been in the military service —

That the said Jas I owns a farm in said county
and State, on which there are three able bodied field
hands, and there is no white male adult on said
farm, and the scarcity of men in this locality
renders it impossible for her to procure the services
of any one to attend to the said farm and hands

That She is willing and able to comply
with the detail of agriculturists, and would
ask that the said Jas I. be detailed
for the detail of agriculturists, and would
ask that the said Jas I. be detailed to
the said farm and hands provided by the late act of Con[gress]

Sworn to and signed   Sarah   [mark]
before me Aug 31st 1864   Launder
W.B. Saunders J.P.

The State of Alabama }
Pickens County }
and A.B. M[...]
the Peace in and [...]
form of la[...]
made by [...]
they a[...]

FROM A LOVE
of HISTORY

THE A. S. WILLIAMS III AMERICANA
COLLECTION AT THE
UNIVERSITY OF ALABAMA

II.
CREATING A NEW NATION: PRESIDENTS, FOUNDING FATHERS, AND FINANCING A NEW NATION

Le Général Washington, Ne Quid Detrimenti Capitat Res publica (1780).

This rare engraving of George Washington was issued in Paris in 1780 by the French engraver Noel Le Mire. It is based on a painting by French artist Jean Baptiste Le Paon after a "tableau" belonging to the Marquis de Lafayette. Its similarities to the figure of Washington in the famous 1776 portrait by Charles Wilson Peale would indicate that Lafayette owned a copy and likely took it to Paris on a trip there in 1779–1780. The African American depicted to the right is William Lee, one of Washington's slaves. Washington once wrote that Lee "followed my fortunes through the war with fidelity." A companion print of Lafayette was also issued by the two artists.

LE GÉNÉRAL WASHINGTON
Ne Quid Detrimenti capiat Res publica.

THE PRESIDENTIAL COLLECTION is the result of Steve Williams's earliest interest in US history. This chapter will represent his initial interest in the Founding Fathers, the struggles of the Revolutionary period, the establishment of our fledgling Republic, and the early US presidents. The formation of this collection eventually led to the comprehensive collecting of the items related to all presidents and their administrations. This collection is supported by a significant collection of books relating to the Founding Fathers, other important statesmen, and the early history of the country. The collection also reflects Williams's fascination with the financing of the Revolution and the early Republic. The financial history collection contains lottery tickets, currency, bills of exchange, as well as documents relating to the financiers themselves.

The genesis of the presidential collection, as previously mentioned, was a day trip to Colonial Williamsburg. The restoration of Virginia's colonial capital, with its pivotal role in the shaping of the history of the Revolutionary period and later, sparked an interest in Williams that has never waned. "I became fascinated with what had been accomplished by these men—Washington, Jefferson, and Adams—in their struggle to create a model republic, so to speak. And I was awed by their brilliance and tenacity in creating the foundation of this great nation."

To that end Williams began collecting books about the early presidents, but that quickly gave way to forming a comprehensive collection around all the men who had served in that capacity. Books written by the presidents, books belonging to or signed by them, and books about them and their administrations were acquired. Books written by and autographed by the presidents are numerous. There is at least one book authored by Grover Cleveland, Theodore Roosevelt, Woodrow Wilson, Calvin Coolidge, and Herbert Hoover. Franklin Delano Roosevelt, Harry Truman, Dwight D. Eisenhower, John F. Kennedy, Lyndon B. Johnson, Richard Nixon, Gerald Ford, Jimmy Carter, Ronald Reagan, and George H. W. Bush are also represented by at least one volume. There are a small number of books owned by presidents, including a copy of John Melish's *A Geographical Description of the United States, with the Contiguous British and Spanish Possessions* presented by Melish to Thomas Jefferson. There are books or pamphlets owned by Andrew Johnson, Millard Fillmore, Chester A. Arthur, and Grover Cleveland.

The book collection subsequently stimulated an interest in documents signed by the presidents. The Williams Collection holds at least one document signed by every president through George W. Bush, including four by James Madison; three by George Washington, Thomas Jefferson, John Quincy Adams, and Abraham Lincoln; and two by John Adams. Two of the more interesting groupings involve

members of the American military. John Porter McCown, a West Point graduate and subsequently a Confederate general, is represented by commissions signed by Martin Van Buren, John Tyler, James K. Polk, and Millard Fillmore. There is also an 1846 letter from Zachary Taylor recommending McCown for a position in a newly formed mounted regiment. Naval officer Alfred W. Hinds's commissions as he moved up the ranks are signed by Grover Cleveland, William McKinley, and Theodore Roosevelt. Hinds's appointment as governor of Guam in 1913 is signed by Woodrow Wilson.

Eleven signers of the Declaration of Independence are represented in the collection, including Charles Carroll, Benjamin Harrison, Samuel Huntington, George Ross, Roger Sherman, William Williams, James Wilson, and Oliver Wolcott. Items signed by John Hancock, William Whipple, and Robert Morris are shown in the following chapter.

There are also documents relating to important figures of the Revolutionary and early national periods such as Aaron Burr, Alexander and Elizabeth Hamilton, Gouverneur Morris, Patrick Henry, Nicholas Biddle, and Peyton Randolph, as well as Samuel Houston, James Wilkinson, and naval heroes Thomas Truxtun and Esek Hopkins.

AUTOGRAPH ALBUM OF THE TWENTY-EIGHTH CONGRESS FROM THE SESSION OF 1844–1845.

This book belonged to Representative Absalom Harris Chappell (1801–1878) of Georgia. Chappell served in the Georgia legislature before being elected to the US House in 1843, replacing John B. Lamar after his resignation. Chappell again served in the state senate after not seeking reelection to the House of Representatives. He was the author of *Miscellanies of Georgia: Historical, Biographical, Descriptive, Etc. . . .* published in Atlanta in 1874. Chappell died in Columbus, Georgia, and is buried there.

The album was left to Chappell's kinsman Thomas J. Chappell who presented it to Georgia historian Charles Edgeworth Jones in 1895. Prominent signers include John Quincy Adams (twice), Alexander H. Stephens, Stephen A. Douglas, Andrew Johnson, and Hannibal Hamlin.

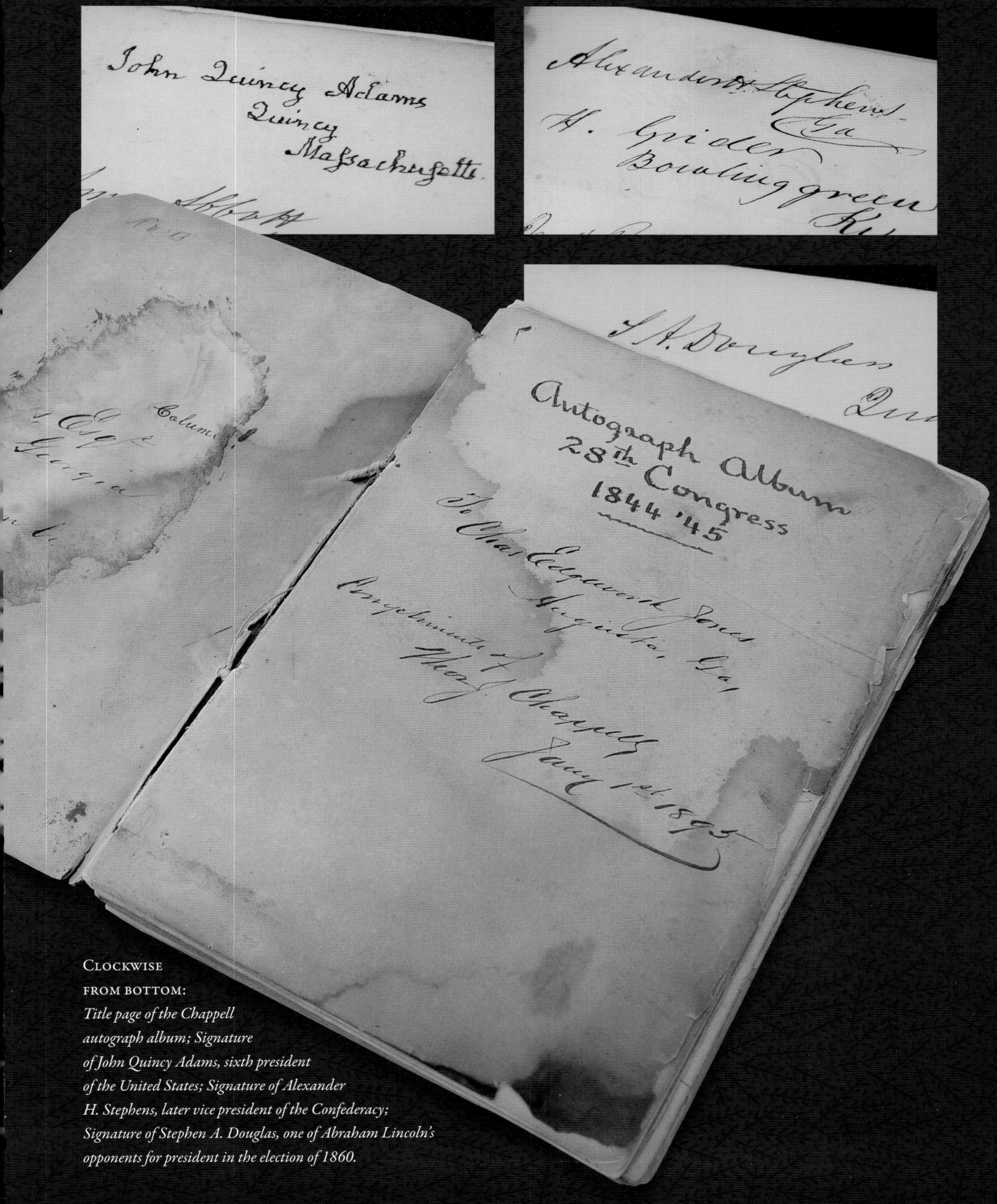

John Quincy Adams
Quincy
Massachusetts

Alexander H. Stephens.
Ga
H. Grider
Bowlinggreen
Ky

S. A. Douglas

Autograph Album
28th Congress
1844 '45

To Chas Edgeworth Jones
Augusta, Ga,
Compliments of
Theo. J. Chappell
Jany 1st 1895

Columbus,
Georgia

A 1765 LOTTERY TICKET FOR THE REBUILDING OF BOSTON'S FANEUIL HALL, BOLDLY SIGNED (AS WAS CUSTOMARY) BY JOHN HANCOCK.

The building, erected in 1742, burned to the ground in 1761, and was rebuilt in 1763. This lottery was apparently one of several held to retire the construction debt. Town hall meetings here from 1764 to 1774, many led by Samuel Adams in opposition to British colonial policies, caused Faneuil Hall to be nicknamed the "Cradle of Liberty."

John Hancock (1737–1793) was one of the foremost leaders of the Revolution. A protégé of Samuel Adams, Hancock became one of the most notable patriots from Massachusetts. As president of the Continental Congress from 1775 to 1777, he received the distinction of being the first signer of the Declaration of Independence. Twice governor of Massachusetts after the establishment of independence, Hancock, along with Adams, was instrumental in Massachusetts narrowly ratifying the US Constitution in 1788.

LOTTERY TICKET SIGNED BY GEORGE WASHINGTON ENTITLING THE HOLDER TO A PRIZE IN THE MOUNTAIN ROAD LOTTERY.

This project was conceived in 1767 by Washington, Captain Thomas Bullitt, and others. Bullitt had served under Washington in the French and Indian War and had been twice recommended for promotion. His rearguard action after Major General James Grant's defeat at the hands of the French in September of 1757 saved the balance of the command from capture. Bullitt and Washington had been subscribers to a land speculation scheme called the Mississippi Company formed in June 1763. The two envisioned a resort or spa at Warm Springs in Augusta County, Virginia (now Bath County), and advertised the sale of tickets in Williamsburg's *Virginia Gazette*. There were to be six thousand tickets sold at a cost of one pound each.

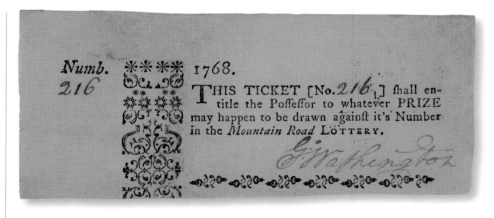

Officially called the Warm Springs Mountain Road Lottery the venture failed for several reasons. Foremost was the large number of lotteries vying for the public's money as well as the banning of all lotteries by George III in 1769. Bullitt persevered however and eventually built the road and spa in Hot Springs, Virginia. This operation eventually became the well-renowned Homestead Resort and Spa.

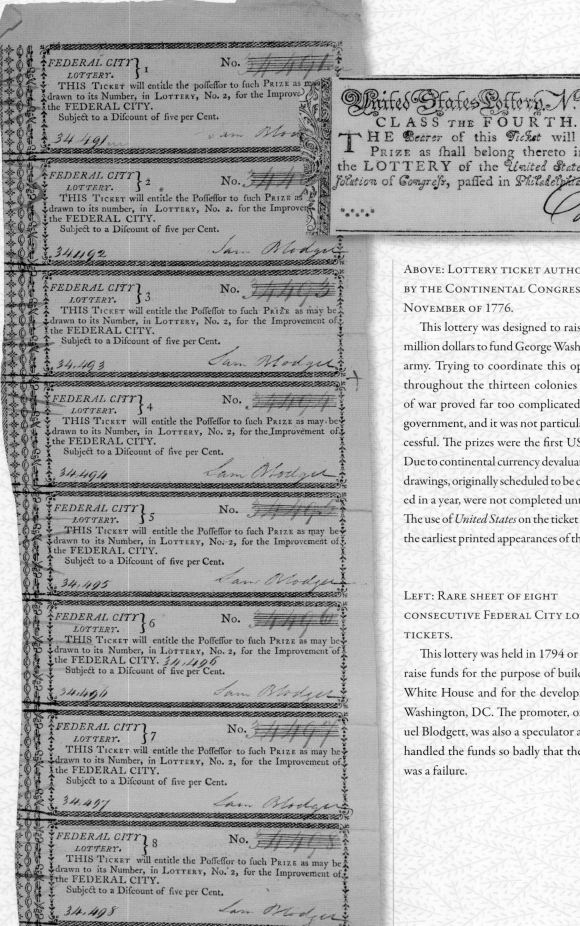

FEDERAL CITY } 1
LOTTERY.
No.
THIS Ticket will entitle the poſſeſſor to such PRIZE as may be drawn to its Number, in LOTTERY, No. 2, for the Improvement of the FEDERAL CITY.
Subject to a Diſcount of five per Cent.

34,491

FEDERAL CITY } 2
LOTTERY.
No.
THIS Ticket will entitle the Poſſeſſor to such PRIZE as may be drawn to its number, in LOTTERY, No. 2. for the Improvement of the FEDERAL CITY.
Subject to a Diſcount of five per Cent.

34,492

FEDERAL CITY } 3
LOTTERY.
No.
THIS Ticket will entitle the Poſſeſſor to such PRIZE as may be drawn to its Number, in LOTTERY, No. 2, for the Improvement of the FEDERAL CITY.
Subject to a Diſcount of five per Cent.

34,493

FEDERAL CITY } 4
LOTTERY.
No.
THIS Ticket will entitle the Poſſeſſor to such PRIZE as may be drawn to its Number, in LOTTERY, No. 2, for the Improvement of the FEDERAL CITY.
Subject to a Diſcount of five per Cent.

34,494

FEDERAL CITY } 5
LOTTERY.
No.
THIS Ticket will entitle the Poſſeſſor to such PRIZE as may be drawn to its Number, in LOTTERY, No. 2, for the Improvement of the FEDERAL CITY.
Subject to a Diſcount of five per Cent.

34,495

FEDERAL CITY } 6
LOTTERY.
No.
THIS Ticket will entitle the Poſſeſſor to such PRIZE as may be drawn to its Number, in LOTTERY, No. 2, for the Improvement of the FEDERAL CITY. 34,496
Subject to a Diſcount of five per Cent.

34,496

FEDERAL CITY } 7
LOTTERY.
No.
THIS Ticket will entitle the Poſſeſſor to such PRIZE as may be drawn to its Number, in LOTTERY, No. 2, for the Improvement of the FEDERAL CITY.
Subject to a Diſcount of five per Cent.

34,497

FEDERAL CITY } 8
LOTTERY.
No.
THIS Ticket will entitle the Poſſeſſor to such PRIZE as may be drawn to its Number, in LOTTERY, No. 2, for the Improvement of the FEDERAL CITY.
Subject to a Diſcount of five per Cent.

34,498

United States Lottery. No 33m802
CLASS THE FOURTH.
THE Bearer of this Ticket will be entitled to such PRIZE as ſhall belong thereto in the Fourth Claſs of the LOTTERY of the United States, agreeable to a Reſolution of Congreſs, paſſed in Philadelphia Novr 18, 1776.
Delany

ABOVE: LOTTERY TICKET AUTHORIZED BY THE CONTINENTAL CONGRESS IN NOVEMBER OF 1776.

This lottery was designed to raise over a million dollars to fund George Washington's army. Trying to coordinate this operation throughout the thirteen colonies in time of war proved far too complicated for the government, and it was not particularly successful. The prizes were the first US bonds. Due to continental currency devaluation, the drawings, originally scheduled to be completed in a year, were not completed until 1782. The use of *United States* on the ticket is one of the earliest printed appearances of that term.

LEFT: RARE SHEET OF EIGHT CONSECUTIVE FEDERAL CITY LOTTERY TICKETS.

This lottery was held in 1794 or 1795 to raise funds for the purpose of building the White House and for the development of Washington, DC. The promoter, one Samuel Blodgett, was also a speculator and mishandled the funds so badly that the lottery was a failure.

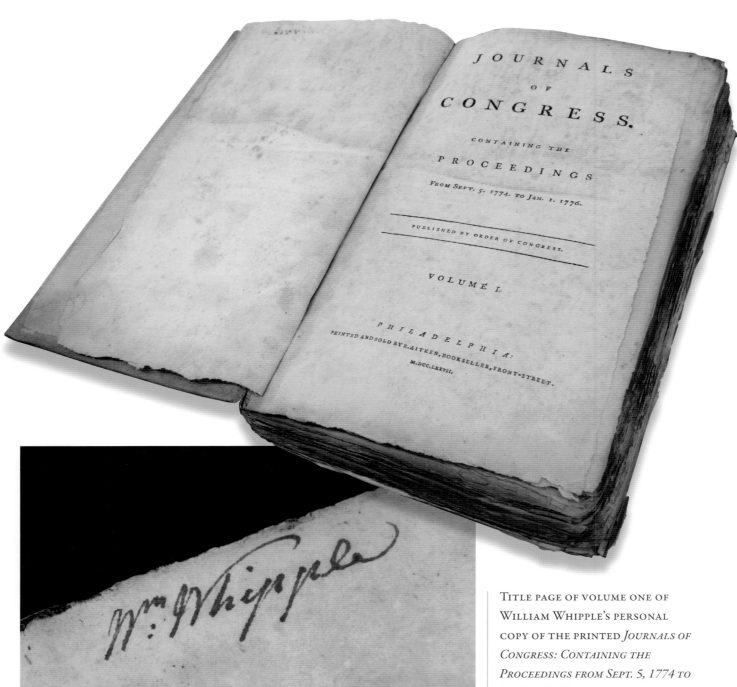

JOURNALS

OF

CONGRESS.

CONTAINING THE
PROCEEDINGS

FROM SEPT. 5, 1774. TO JAN. 1. 1776.

PUBLISHED BY ORDER OF CONGRESS.

VOLUME I.

PHILADELPHIA:
PRINTED AND SOLD BY R. AITKEN, BOOKSELLER, FRONT-STREET.
M.DCC.LXXVII.

SIGNATURE OF WILLIAM WHIPPLE, SIGNER OF THE DECLARATION OF INDEPENDENCE, IN HIS SET OF THE *JOURNALS OF THE CONTINENTAL CONGRESS.*

Whipple (1730–1785) was a delegate to the provincial congresses from New Hampshire. His first career, that of a sailor and ship's master, found him incidentally involved in the slave trade, still legal at that time. Sent as a delegate to the Continental Congress in 1776, he served in that body un-til 1779, taking time out to serve in the field at Saratoga and in the campaign in Rhode Island. One source indicates that he freed his slave Prince Whipple because he felt he could not fight for liberty and freedom and own a slave. An effective member of Congress and a true patriot, his correspondence expressed an exasperation with "the lack of national spirit and the greed and selfishness of leaders and communities." His postwar years were spent as an associate justice of the superior court of New Hampshire.

TITLE PAGE OF VOLUME ONE OF WILLIAM WHIPPLE'S PERSONAL COPY OF THE PRINTED *JOURNALS OF CONGRESS: CONTAINING THE PROCEEDINGS FROM SEPT. 5, 1774 TO JAN. 1, 1776* (PHILADELPHIA: PRINTED BY R. AITKEN, BOOKSELLER, 1777).

The Williams collection also includes Whipple's copy of the second volume of the journals, which covers the period from January 1, 1776, to January 1, 1777, and was printed in York-Town, Pennsylvania, in 1778.

RARE SHEET OF NATIONAL CURRENCY ISSUED BY THE CONTINENTAL CONGRESS IN 1779.

The denominations range from thirty to seventy-five dollars and are redeemable in "Spanish milled Dollars, or an equal sum in Gold or Silver."

1782 letter from Robert Morris to John Hopkins.

The financing of the American Revolution was an involved process, and subsequent interest payments on the war debt accumulated by the new nation made heavy demands on the federal treasury. The failure of various states to pay federal tax requisitions was especially troubling to Superintendent of Finance Robert Morris, the man responsible for making payments on loan obligations, most notably to France. In 1782 Morris sent this letter to John Hopkins, continental loan officer for the state of Virginia (as well as officers of the remaining states), suspending payment of transatlantic interest payments on US debt obligations. Morris knew that France had already authorized a new loan but hoped to bring pressure on the delinquent states. The plan backfired as several states voted to make the interest payments, on paper at least, from state funds. Morris was forced to begin making federal interest payments again in 1784. A noted scholar of the financing of the Revolution considers this letter as documentation of "the first and only intentional default of United States government obligations."

Robert Morris (1734–1806) was a signer of the Declaration of Independence, the Articles of Confederation, and the US Constitution. Active in Pennsylvania Revolutionary politics, he was also a delegate to the Second Continental Congress from 1775 to 1778. A prominent Philadelphia merchant, Morris was a central figure in matters regarding trade and economics during these years. Utilizing his extensive international trading contacts and financial acumen for the benefit of the country, he has been called the Financier of the Revolution. From 1781 to 1784 Morris was superintendent of finance for the United States. Though his personal interests were occasionally intertwined with those of the government, he performed the unenviable tasks of borrowing money for the prosecution of the war and keeping Washington's army supplied. During his tenure the Bank of North America was founded, with a substantial loan from France, for the purpose of financing the struggle for independence.

Morris was George Washington's choice to be the first secretary of the treasury, but Morris declined, urging the appointment of Alexander Hamilton, who shared many of his views on financial policy. In a typical gesture Morris rented his house in Philadelphia to the city for a small sum with the proviso that it be used as the President's House while it was the nation's capital. Between 1790 and 1800 both Washington and John Adams resided there.

Morris's postwar career involved some unsuccessful land speculations (at one time he owned more land than any other American, something over six million acres, but had little in the way of monetary assets). His creditors caused him to be sent to debtor's prison in Philadelphia in 1798. The Bankruptcy Act of 1800 gave him relief from his debts, and he spent his remaining years in retirement.

COMMISSION SIGNED BY PATRICK HENRY AS GOVERNOR OF VIRGINIA ON JUNE 23, 1785, APPOINTING JAMES BATES JR. AN ENSIGN IN THE MILITIA OF HALIFAX COUNTY.

Patrick Henry (1736–1799) was a brilliant orator who led Virginia's opposition to unfair royal taxes in the period leading up to the Revolution. His opposition to the Stamp Act in 1765 led the Virginia House of Burgesses to pass the Virginia Stamp Act Resolutions. These resolves are considered by some historians to be a major catalyst of colonial opposition to Parliamentary taxation. They affirmed the exclusive right of the colonial assemblies to self-taxation and further affirmed that the right could not be assigned to other governing bodies.

With the outbreak of the Revolution seemingly unavoidable, the Virginia House of Burgesses met in Richmond in March of 1775. Under discussion was the possible mobilization of the militia to counter any British military incursion. Henry swayed the burgesses to mobilize with his immortal "Give me Liberty, or Give me Death!" speech. After a brief period of military service Henry was elected the first postcolonial governor of Virginia, serving from July 5, 1776, to June 1, 1779.

Henry was again elected governor in 1784 and served until 1786. He was vocal in his opposition to the US Constitution; in his consideration it gave too much power to the federal government at the expense of state rights. With its ratification Henry became an ardent supporter of the addition of the Bill of Rights as amendments to the Constitution. George Washington offered Henry the position of secretary of state in 1795. His refusal at that time was due to his opposition to Washington's Federalist policies, but as time passed, Henry came to be more in line with the policies of Washington and John Adams. An appointment in 1798 by Adams to be special emissary to France was declined by Henry only due to his failing health.

BROADSIDE PRINTING SIGNED BY THOMAS JEFFERSON AS SECRETARY OF STATE.

The broadside is a 1793 congressional act "relative to Claims against the United States, not barred by any act of Limitation, and which have not already been adjusted."

LEFT: *A contemporary engraved portrait of Jefferson.*

Treasury Department
September 6. 1792.

Sir

It has been stated to me by Messrs Oliver and Thomson that the Ship Eliza, N Stone Master, entered at Alexandria in November last, and proceeded up the River in <u>Ballast</u> to load at George Town, where the said Master had been obliged to pay Tonnage a second time.

If the case is accurately stated, and the Master had paid Tonnage at Alexandria, as may be inferred from the entry said to have been made there, your charge was erro=neously made, and the Tonnage Duty paid to you must in that case be refunded.

I am, Sir,
Your Obed Servant.
Alexander Hamilton

James M Lingan Esqr
George Town.

LETTER SIGNED BY ALEXANDER HAMILTON TO JAMES M. LINGAN, HEADLINED "TREASURY DEPARTMENT, SEPTEMBER 6, 1792."

The letter is the the duty on the ship *Eliza,* which had been double charged, and instructs Lingan to refund the fee charged at George Town (now Georgetown, DC) inasmuch as the duty had been paid at Alexandria, Virginia.

Alexander Hamilton (1757–1804) was the first secretary of the treasury, holding that office from 1789 to 1795. He was coauthor of *The Federalist Papers* and the primary author of the new nation's economic policies, including the establishment of a national bank and giving the federal government more authority in fiscal matters generally. Hamilton was killed in a duel with political opponent Aaron Burr.

AUTOGRAPH LETTER OF ELIZABETH SCHUYLER HAMILTON (1757–1854) DATED JANUARY 29, 1830, TO JACOB MORRIS.

Elizabeth Hamilton was the daughter of Philip Schuyler, a general in the American army during the Revolution. She married Alexander Hamilton in 1780 and became his devoted partner until his death in 1804; they had eight children together. Elizabeth overlooked Alexander's infidelities and carried on a feud with James Monroe regarding charges he made against Hamilton over some financial irregularities, later refusing Monroe's apology over the incident. Apparently left in limited means after Hamilton's death, this letter to Jacob Morris asks for a payment due of two hundred dollars, saying "if it could be sent shortly it would be very convenient."

My good Sir

Your last letter informed me that a further payment was to be made me of two hundred Dollars if it could be sent me shortly it would be very convenient, I hope your family are all well when you visit your friends in my neighbourhood it would give me pleasure to see you or any of your family that accompanys you I have room enough to accommodate you with great regard. Eliz Hamilton

Near New York
Grange January 29th, 1830.
Mr Jacob Morris.

JOHN ADAMS, PPESIDENT *of the* UNITED STATES *of* AMERICA,

To all who shall see these Presents, Greeting :

Know Ye, THAT in pursuance of an Act of Congress of the United States in this case provided, passed on the ninth day of July, one thousand seven hundred and ninety-eight, I have commissioned, and by these presents do commission the private armed *Schooner* called the *Scorpion* of the burthen of *one hundred seventy* tons, or thereabouts, owned by *Samuel Walker* ~~~~~~~~ *of the City of Baltimore in the State of Maryland Merchants*

mounting *six* carriage guns, and navigated by *Ten* men ; hereby licensing and authorizing *Peter Sorenson* captain, and *Edw: Fitzgerrald and Nicholas Nowlan* lieutenants of the said *Schooner* and the other officers and crew thereof to subdue, seize and take any armed French vessel which shall be found within the jurisdictional limits of ti   ewhere on the high seas ; and such captured vessel, with her apparel, guns and ap   ods or effects which shall be found on board the same, together with all French persons and others, who shall be found   g on board, to bring within some port of the United States ; and also to retake any   oods and effects of the people of the United States, which may have been captured by any French armed vessel ; in order that proceedings may be had concerning such capture or re-capture in due form of law, and as to right and justice shall appertain. This commission to continue in force during the pleasure of the President of the United States for the time being.

GIVEN *under my Hand and the Seal of the United States of America, at Philadelphia, the seventh day of December in the year of our Lord, one thousand seven hundred and ninety nine and of the Independence of the said States, the twenty fourth.*

John Adams

By the President,

Timothy Pickering Secretary of State.

PRIVATEER'S COMMISSION SIGNED BY JOHN ADAMS AS PRESIDENT, PHILADELPHIA, DECEMBER 7, 1799.

The six-gun schooner *Scorpion*, owned by Samuel Walker of Baltimore and captained by one Peter Sorenson, was authorized by this document to "subdue, seize and take any armed French vessel" and if possible bring it to an American port. The *Scorpion* was a participant in the "Quasi-War" between the United States and the French Republic from 1798 to 1800. Though undeclared, it was an effort by the United States to curb the depredations of French naval privateers on American shipping. In addition to the US Navy, Adams commissioned 365 privateers. The French, after losing over a hundred privateers, agreed to a cessation of hostilities.

Sir   Richmond May 1st 1800.

In 1795, seventy two stands of Arms were delivered to Captain James Caruthers, for the use of his company of Light Infantry belonging to the 8th Regiment of militia. Under a late regulation it is indispensably necessary that those Arms be retaken into the hands of the Government that they may be repaired and afterwards distributed as the law directs. I have therefore to request that you will immediately take into your possession those arms and apprize me of it as soon as you have done so, noting particularly their situation. Should any of these Arms be lost, which it is hoped is not the case, you will be pleased to state by whom and by what means, that the publick may be indemnified where it is practicable.

With great respect I am sir,
Your obd^t Servant
Jas Monroe

Lt Col^l James McDowell

Rockbridge

Monroe wrote to Colonel James McDowell regarding the return to the state of seventy-two muskets issued to a unit in the Virginia militia in 1795 for repair and reissuance.

FACING PAGE: APPOINTMENT OF NICOL FORDIEK OF CONNECTICUT AS A FEDERAL BANKRUPTCY COMMISSIONER, DATED JULY 6, 1802, AND SIGNED BY JAMES MADISON AS SECRETARY OF STATE.

Fordiek was appointed along with eleven other individuals under the Bankruptcy Act of 1800. This was the first such act passed by Congress and did much to relieve the debts of a number of prominent Revolutionary War patriots who had experienced financial reverses after independence. The most notable of this group included Robert Morris, William Duer, and John Nicholson. The act was repealed in 1803, and it would be thirty-eight years before another was passed, this in response to the economic crash of 1837.

DEPARTMENT OF STATE.

July 6 - 1802

SIR,

IN pursuance of an Act of the last Session of Congress, authorising the President of the United States to appoint COMMISSIONERS OF BANK-RUPTCY in the several districts composing the United States, he has selected yourself together with *Hezekiah Huntington, Jonathan Bull, Joseph Hart, John Dodd, Henry W Edwards, Elihu Munson Jehosaphat Starr, John Nichol, Elisha Hyde, Jonathan Frisbie and Jacob DeWitt* —————

————— ESQUIRES, to be COMMISSIONERS for the District of *Connecticut* —————; and I have the pleasure herewith to enclose your commission.

I am, very respectfully,

Sir,

Your obedient servant,

James Madison

Nichol Fottick Esq

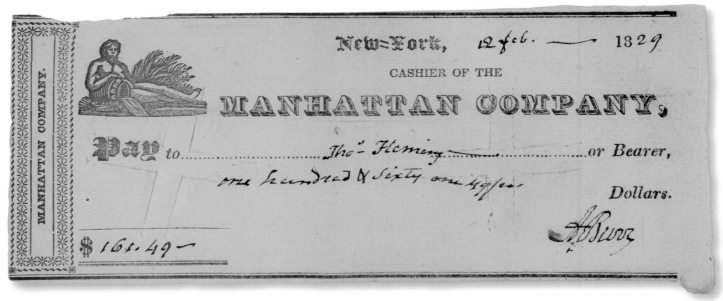

CASHIER OF THE

MANHATTAN COMPANY,

New=York, 12 feb. 1829

Pay to.................Tho.ˢ Fleming.................or Bearer,

one hundred & sixty one 49/100

Dollars.

$161.49

MANHATTAN COMPANY.

CHECK DRAWN ON THE MANHATTAN COMPANY OF NEW YORK ON FEBRUARY 12, 1829, TO ONE THOMAS FLEMING IN THE AMOUNT OF $161.49 AND SIGNED BY AARON BURR.

One of the more enigmatic of the Founding Fathers, Burr (1756–1836) is known primarily for his famous duel with Alexander Hamilton and his trial for treason. He was also a brilliant lawyer, a more than competent soldier, a US senator, and the third vice president of the United States. Narrowly defeated for president in 1800, he was at political odds with Jefferson and Hamilton for the balance of their careers.

The Manhattan Company was a scheme of Burr's to allow him to create a bank, which under New York law and the watchful eye of Hamilton was a formidable task. Burr initially convinced Hamilton that the sole business of the company was to bring fresh water to New York City. Hamilton approved this concept and backed Burr in this endeavor. The bill passed by the New York legislature in 1799 contained a provision that allowed the company to utilize its surplus capital in other endeavors. Burr circumvented Hamilton's opposition to state banks in this manner, and the Manhattan Company became the predecessor to JPMorgan Chase.

FACING PAGE: SIGNATURE OF ANDREW JACKSON AS PRESIDENT ON AN UNISSUED DOCUMENT AUTHORIZING THE OPERATION OF A SHIP UNDER US LAW PROVIDED THE OWNER IS A US CITIZEN.

Presidents actually signed such documents, including federal appointments and military commissions, well into the twentieth century. This document is also signed by one Anthony Suskind as acting secretary of state. There were four different secretaries of state during Jackson's presidency, and James Alexander Hamilton is listed as acting secretary of state in March of 1829. Interestingly, Suskind is not included on a list of acting secretaries of state.

By the President of the United States of America

SUFFER the

master or commander of the burthen of

tons or thereabouts mounted with

guns navigated with men

TO PASS with her Company Passengers

Goods and Merchandize without any hinderance seisure or molestation

the said appearing by good testimony to belong to one

or more of the Citizens of the United States and to him or them only

Given under my Hand and the Seal of the

United States of America the

Number

day of in the year of our Lord

thousand hundred and

Andrew Jackson

By the President

Asbury Dickins, acting Secretary of State

State of

District of

To all Persons whom
these may concern

Countersigned by

ABOVE: WEST POINT DIPLOMA OF
CADET JOHN PORTER MCCOWN.

McCown graduated in July of 1840, tenth in a class of forty-two. The diploma is signed by Richard Delafield as commandant and Dennis Hart Mahan as professor of engineering. McCown was promoted to second lieutenant on July 25, 1840, and assigned to the Fourth Artillery, that commission being signed by Martin Van Buren. McCown's promotion to first lieutenant on January 18, 1844, was signed by John Tyler. During the Mexican War McCown was distinguished with a brevet captaincy for his gallant conduct at the battle of Cerro Gordo. That document is signed by James K. Polk.

BELOW: AUTOGRAPH LETTER BY
ZACHARY TAYLOR, WRITTEN IN
1846, RECOMMENDING MCCOWN
IN GLOWING TERMS FOR AN
APPOINTMENT TO ONE OF THE TWO
REGIMENTS OF MOUNTED RIFLES
THEN BEING FORMED.

Taylor characterizes McCown as "temperate, hardy & discreet; a good woodsman & hunter." Taylor goes on to say that if McCown is selected "I have no hesitation in saying that he will discharge all the duties ... with zeal & ability." McCown's commission promoting him to the permanent rank of captain was signed by Millard Fillmore on March 12, 1851. McCown went on to join the Confederacy in 1861 and was ultimately promoted to major general. After a falling out with General Braxton Bragg, he was court-martialed in 1863 and spent the balance of the war in obscurity.

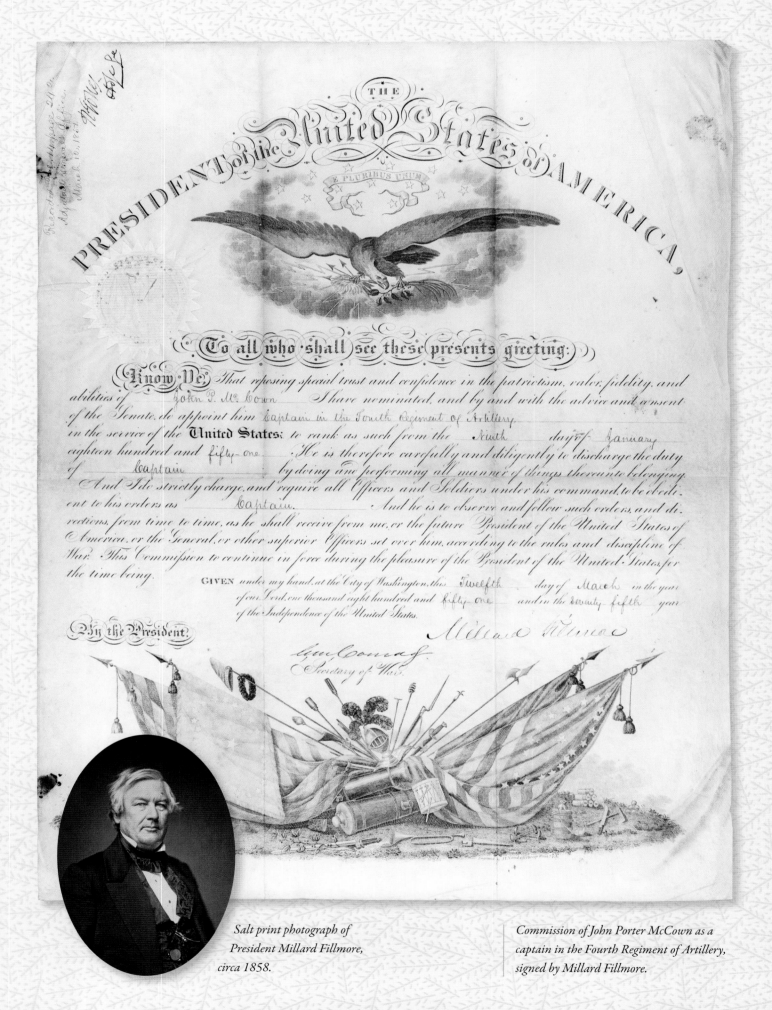

THE

PRESIDENT of the United States of AMERICA,

E PLURIBUS UNUM

To all who shall see these presents greeting:

Know Ye, That reposing special trust and confidence in the patriotism, valor, fidelity, and abilities of *John P. McCown* I have nominated, and by and with the advice and consent of the Senate, do appoint him *Captain in the Fourth Regiment of Artillery*, in the service of the **United States**: to rank as such from the *Ninth* day of *January* eighteen hundred and *fifty-one*. He is therefore carefully and diligently to discharge the duty of *Captain* by doing and performing all manner of things thereunto belonging. And I do strictly charge, and require all Officers and Soldiers under his command, to be obedient to his orders as *Captain*. And he is to observe and follow such orders, and directions, from time to time, as he shall receive from me, or the future President of the United States of America, or the General, or other superior Officers set over him, according to the rules and discipline of War. This Commission to continue in force during the pleasure of the President of the United States, for the time being. GIVEN under my hand, at the City of Washington, this *Twelfth* day of *March* in the year of our Lord, one thousand eight hundred and *fifty-one* and in the *seventy-fifth* year of the Independence of the United States.

By the President:

Millard Fillmore

Geo. Conrad
Secretary of War.

Salt print photograph of
President Millard Fillmore,
circa 1858.

Commission of John Porter McCown as a
captain in the Fourth Regiment of Artillery,
signed by Millard Fillmore.

AUTOGRAPH LETTER SIGNED BY PRESIDENT ABRAHAM LINCOLN TO SIMON CAMERON AND DATED NOVEMBER 6, 1863.

Cameron (1799–1889) was Lincoln's first secretary of war but was forced to resign on January 14, 1862. He served as minister to Russia until the fall of 1862, at which time he went home to Pennsylvania, remaining out of politics until 1866. The nature of the trials mentioned in the letter is unclear, but Lincoln involved a member of the US attorney general's office on behalf of Cameron, then a private citizen. Lincoln writes: "It might do good, for the government to *urge* for the trials, whether it should succeed in bringing them on or not." Thirteen days later the president would deliver the Gettysburg Address.

October 24, 1902.

My dear Judge Jones:

I shall keep the copy of Stonewall Jackson because it has your name on it; but what I shall do with it is to supplant by it a copy now in my library.   I have always been greatly interested in this study of Jackson by Henderson.   I have been anxious that Henderson should make a further study of Lee, and wrote him to this effect. Practically, these two volumes contain what I regard as on the whole *an excellent* *a really admirable* history of the first two years of the war in the east.   I wish he would supplement it by Lee's life, which would give us the last two.

With high regard,

Faithfully yours,

Theodore Roosevelt

Hon. Thomas G. Jones,
    U. S. District Judge,
        Huntsville, Alabama.

TYPED LETTER SIGNED BY THEODORE ROOSEVELT TO JUDGE THOMAS GOODE JONES OF ALABAMA ON WHITE HOUSE STATIONERY, DATED OCTOBER 24, 1902.

Roosevelt thanks Jones for the gift of a biography of Thomas Jonathan "Stonewall" Jackson by eminent British military historian Colonel G. F. R. Henderson. The first edition was published in two volumes in 1898 and was considered the definitive life of Jackson at that time.

Thomas Goode Jones (1844–1914) was a Confederate officer, federal district judge, and governor of Alabama. Jones attended the Virginia Military Institute from 1859 to 1862, leaving school with his class to serve in the Confederate army. He rose to the rank of major, eventually serving on the staff of General John B. Gordon, and was wounded four times during the war. Admitted to the bar in 1866, Jones was admitted to practice before the US Supreme Court in 1876. Active in local and state politics, he was a member of the Alabama legislature from 1884 to 1888 and was elected governor for two terms beginning in 1890. Jones was elected to the presidency of the Alabama State Bar in 1901 and that same year was appointed to a federal district judgeship by Theodore Roosevelt.

The letter establishes the fact that Roosevelt already had a set of the Jackson biography but intended to keep the set from Jones "because it has your name on it." Roosevelt goes on to say that he has "been anxious that Henderson should make a further study of Lee, and wrote him to this effect." Roosevelt, of course, was greatly interested in American history in general, but his interest in the Civil War was perhaps enhanced by the fact that his mother Martha was a half-sister to James Dunwoody Bulloch (1823–1901). Bulloch was a distinguished US naval officer before the war but in 1861 offered his services to the Confederacy. Posted to England, he was responsible for arranging the building and outfitting of nearly all the Confederate cruising ships, including the C.S.S. *Alabama*.

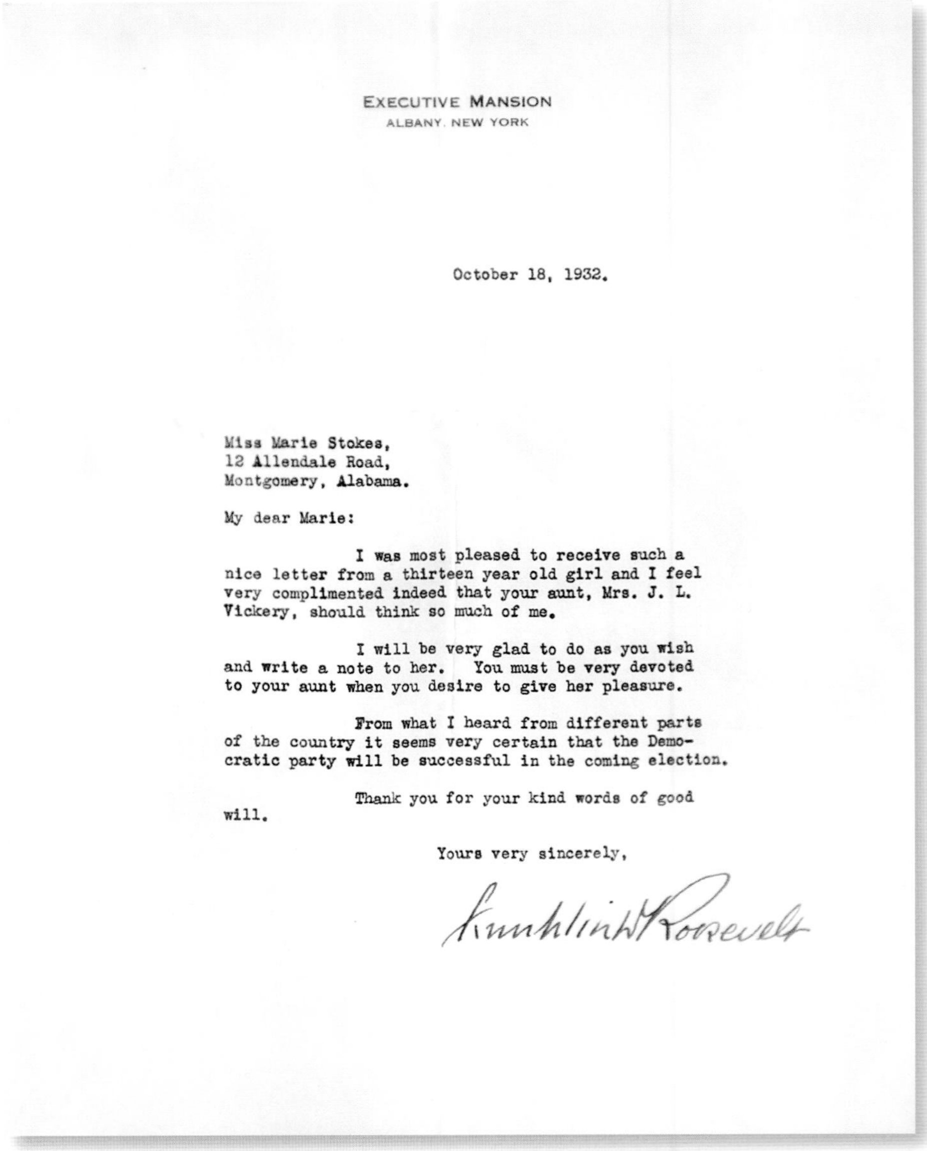

October 18, 1932.

Miss Marie Stokes,
12 Allendale Road,
Montgomery, Alabama.

My dear Marie:

I was most pleased to receive such a nice letter from a thirteen year old girl and I feel very complimented indeed that your aunt, Mrs. J. L. Vickery, should think so much of me.

I will be very glad to do as you wish and write a note to her. You must be very devoted to your aunt when you desire to give her pleasure.

From what I heard from different parts of the country it seems very certain that the Democratic party will be successful in the coming election.

Thank you for your kind words of good will.

Yours very sincerely,

Franklin D. Roosevelt

TYPED LETTER SIGNED BY FRANKLIN DELANO ROOSEVELT TO A MISS MARIE STOKES OF MONTGOMERY, ALABAMA.

Stokes, then thirteen, requested in a previous letter that then Governor Roosevelt write to her aunt, a Mrs. J. L. Vickery. Roosevelt agrees to do so and goes on to say "it seems very certain that the Democratic Party will be successful in the coming election." Roosevelt would be elected our thirty-second president three weeks later.

Signed photograph of Franklin Delano Roosevelt.

THE WHITE HOUSE
WASHINGTON

April 6, 1989

Dear Bill:

It was especially good to have you here for the
swearing-in of Ed Derwinski as Secretary of the
new Department of Veterans Affairs.

As our nation's major cartoonist during World
War II, you buoyed the spirits of our men and
women in uniform with your memorable "Willie and
Joe" cartoons. Thank you for your unique
contribution to that war effort and for your
participation in the recent White House event.

I'm delighted to have the framed print of an
original "Willie and Joe" which you inscribed for
me at the ceremony. It's a wonderful keepsake of
your friendship. Many thanks.

Barbara joins me in wishing you our very best.

Sincerely,

G. Bush

Mr. Bill Mauldin
1110 Old Santa Fe Trail
Santa Fe, New Mexico 87501

TYPED LETTER SIGNED BY PRESIDENT
GEORGE H. W. BUSH ON WHITE HOUSE
LETTERHEAD, DATED APRIL 6, 1989,
TO WILLIAM HENRY "BILL" MAULDIN
(1921–2003).

Mauldin was a World War II infantryman and cartoonist who created the characters of "Willie and Joe," the "everyman"
enlisted soldiers of the American army. A
compilation of these cartoons published in
book form under the title *Up Front* in 1945
won Mauldin the first of two Pulitzer Prizes.

*Signed photograph of Bill Mauldin
presenting a "Willie and Joe" cartoon
portrait to President Bush.*

To Bill Mauldin
With best wishes,
G. Bush

II.
STATE AND REGION: THE HISTORY OF ALABAMA AND THE SOUTH

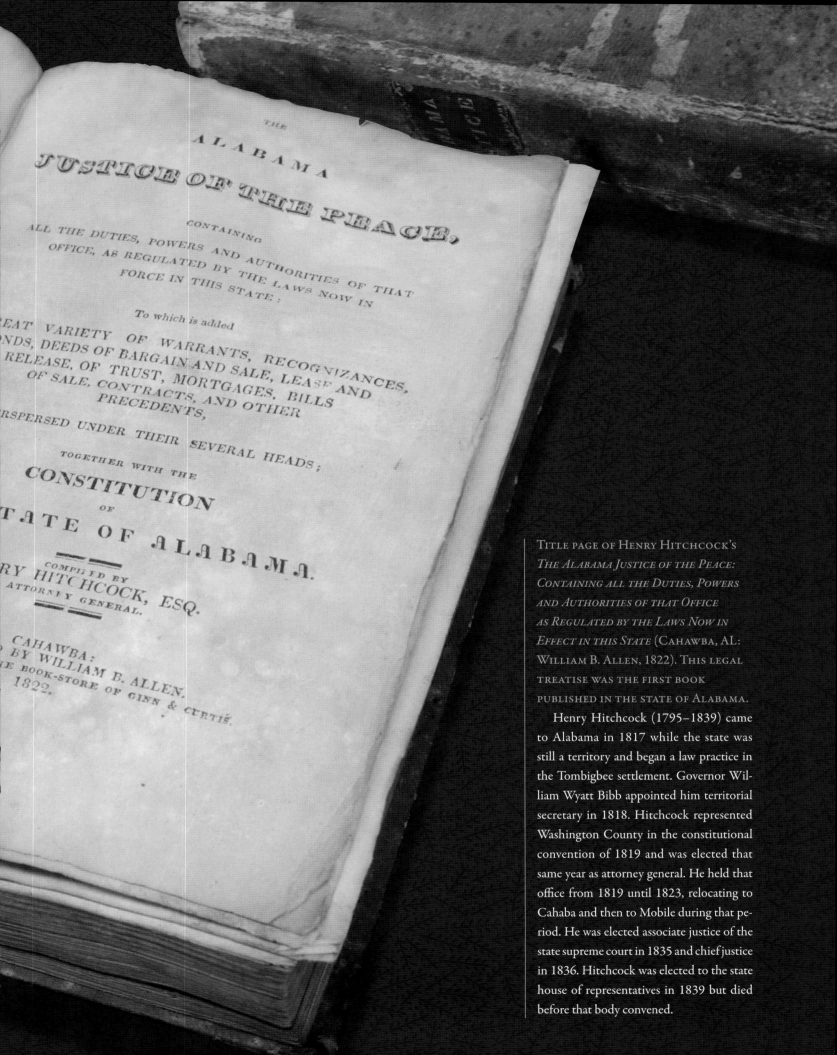

THE
ALABAMA
JUSTICE OF THE PEACE,

CONTAINING

ALL THE DUTIES, POWERS AND AUTHORITIES OF THAT
OFFICE, AS REGULATED BY THE LAWS NOW IN
FORCE IN THIS STATE;

To which is added

[GR]EAT VARIETY OF WARRANTS, RECOGNIZANCES,
[BO]NDS, DEEDS OF BARGAIN AND SALE, LEASE AND
RELEASE, OF TRUST, MORTGAGES, BILLS
OF SALE, CONTRACTS, AND OTHER
PRECEDENTS,

[INTE]RSPERSED UNDER THEIR SEVERAL HEADS;

TOGETHER WITH THE

CONSTITUTION
OF
[S]TATE OF ALABAMA.

COMPILED BY
[HEN]RY HITCHCOCK, ESQ.
ATTORNEY GENERAL.

CAHAWBA:
[PUBLISHE]D BY WILLIAM B. ALLEN.
[AT TH]E BOOK-STORE OF GINN & CURTIS.
1822.

TITLE PAGE OF HENRY HITCHCOCK'S
*The Alabama Justice of the Peace:
Containing all the Duties, Powers
and Authorities of that Office
as Regulated by the Laws Now in
Effect in this State* (Cahawba, AL:
William B. Allen, 1822). This legal
treatise was the first book
published in the state of Alabama.

Henry Hitchcock (1795–1839) came
to Alabama in 1817 while the state was
still a territory and began a law practice in
the Tombigbee settlement. Governor William
Wyatt Bibb appointed him territorial
secretary in 1818. Hitchcock represented
Washington County in the constitutional
convention of 1819 and was elected that
same year as attorney general. He held that
office from 1819 until 1823, relocating to
Cahaba and then to Mobile during that period.
He was elected associate justice of the
state supreme court in 1835 and chief justice
in 1836. Hitchcock was elected to the state
house of representatives in 1839 but died
before that body convened.

A S A NATIVE ALABAMIAN it was only logical that Steve Williams should begin to collect items related to the history and literature of his state along with those related to his larger national interests. His specific interest in Alabama grew to encompass the history of the South. While Alabama was always the primary focus, this portion of the collection advanced from books to maps, photography, manuscripts, and prints. It contains a significant grouping of books related to early travels in the region, primarily from the period from 1750 to 1900. Nineteen of Rucker Agee's *Twenty Alabama Books*, all in the first edition, comprise part of this collection. Additionally the A. S. Williams III Americana Collection houses an important collection of Alabama almanacs.

All of the states that are considered part of the South, as well as the border states of Maryland and Kentucky, are represented in the collection. The trans-Mississippi states of Missouri, Texas, and Arkansas are represented in a small number of rare or important works.

TITLE PAGE OF THE FIRST PRINTING OF WILLIAM STITH'S *THE HISTORY OF THE DISCOVERY AND SETTLEMENT OF VIRGINIA: BEING AN ESSAY TOWARDS A GENERAL HISTORY OF THE COLONY* (WILLIAMSBURG, VA: PRINTED BY WILLIAM PARKS, 1747).

One of the rarest volumes relating to colonial Virginia, this book reflects Williams's interest in the totality of southern history. While the majority of this portion of the collection relates to Alabama history, all of the southern states are well represented with contemporary histories and travel accounts, as well as scholarly monographs and pamphlets.

William Stith (1707–1755) was born in Virginia and educated at Queen's College, Oxford. Ordained as a minister in the Church of England, he returned to Virginia in 1731. He took a position as master of the grammar school attached to the College of William and Mary, and he also served as chaplain to the Virginia House of Burgesses. Stith was called to take charge of Henrico Parish in 1736, remaining there for sixteen years. During his free time he composed his *History*, based on the earlier writings of Captain John Smith and Robert Beverley. A thorough scholar, Stith supplemented their accounts by making use of the official records of the London Company as well as the public papers of his uncle Sir John Randolph. Randolph had held numerous important positions in the colony, including Speaker of the House of Burgesses. Stith accepted the position of president of the College of William and Mary in 1752, becoming the third person to hold that office.

Stith's account is one of the most important early secondary accounts of the history of the colony of Virginia. His consciousness of the importance of Virginia's history and traditions is notable throughout the work. In his personal life Stith was noted for opposition to certain royal attempts to usurp Virginia's rights of self-government.

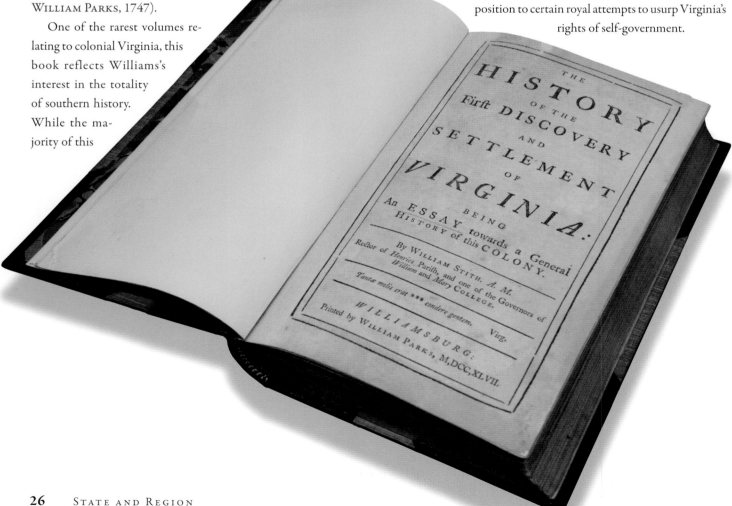

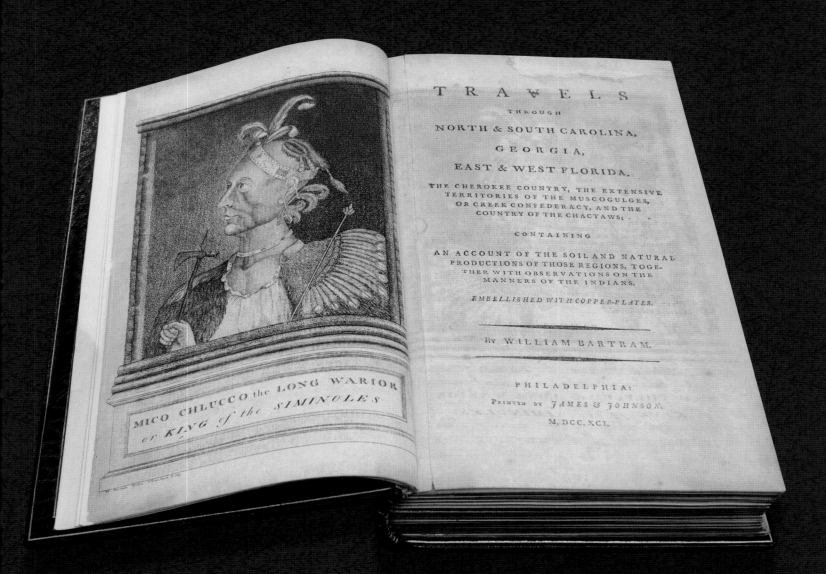

TRAVELS

THROUGH

NORTH & SOUTH CAROLINA,

GEORGIA,

EAST & WEST FLORIDA.

THE CHEROKEE COUNTRY, THE EXTENSIVE
TERRITORIES OF THE MUSCOGULGES,
OR CREEK CONFEDERACY, AND THE
COUNTRY OF THE CHACTAWS;

CONTAINING

AN ACCOUNT OF THE SOIL AND NATURAL
PRODUCTIONS OF THOSE REGIONS, TOGE-
THER WITH OBSERVATIONS ON THE
MANNERS OF THE INDIANS.

EMBELLISHED WITH COPPER-PLATES.

By WILLIAM BARTRAM.

PHILADELPHIA:
PRINTED BY JAMES & JOHNSON.
M,DCC,XCI.

MICO CHLUCCO the LONG WARIOR or KING of the SIMINOLES.

This first American edition is one of the most significant rare books in the Williams Collection. Alabama bibliophile and map collector Rucker Agee included this volume in his *Twenty Alabama Books*. In this 1975 publication Agee compiled what he considered to be the essential books to an understanding of "the evolution of Alabama—from the Spanish conquest to the twentieth century." The Williams Collection holds first editions of nineteen of the twenty titles. Among the rarest titles are the Bartram, *The History of the American Indians . . .* by James Adair originally published in London in 1775, and *Woodward's Reminiscences of the Creek, or Muscogee Indians, Contained in Letters to Friends in Georgia and Alabama . . .* by Thomas S. Woodward published in Montgomery in 1859.

William Bartram (1739–1823) was the son of renowned naturalist and botanist John Bartram (1699–1777). William followed in his father's footsteps and in 1773 embarked on a four-year journey through the southern colonies. Trained as a botanist and nature illustrator, Bartram compiled notes and drawings on the flora and fauna of the region. He was interested in the Native Americans he encountered and spent a portion of the year 1776 in exploring the Cherokee Nation. Several sites in Alabama memorialize Bartram's travels in the region. The William Bartram Arboretum is located within Fort Toulouse Park, near Wetumpka, and the Bartram Canoe Trail can be navigated in the Mobile-Tensaw Delta. The trail, for kayaks and canoes, is operated by the Alabama Department of Conservation.

Secy. of State

THE HALCYON,

And Tombeckbe Public Advertiser.

V·L. VI. ST. STEPHENS, (Alabama) MONDAY, SEPTEMBER 11, 1820. NO. 20.

PRINTED AND PUBLISHED, WEEKLY,

BY THOMAS EASTIN,

PRINTER OF THE LAWS OF THE UNITED STATES

TERMS—*Four Dollars* per annum, payable half-annually in advance.

Advertisements without directions as to the number of insertions, will be continued until forbidden, and charged accordingly.

BY AUTHORITY.

ACTS OF THE SIXTEENTH CONGRESS.

An act for the relief of the legal representatives of Conrad Laub, deceased.

Be it enacted by the Senate and House of Representatives of the United States of America in congress assembled, That the person authorized to transact the business of the late supervisor of the Revenue in the state of Pennsylvania, be, and he is hereby, authorised and directed to revise the accounts of Conrad Laub, deceased, late a collector of Internal Duties in the state aforesaid, and to audit and settle the same, admitting, on sufficient evidence, all legal or equitable credits not heretofore allowed or rejected by Congress.

Sec. 2 *And be it further enacted,* That if the Administrator of the said Conrad Laub, deceased, shall be dissatisfied with the settlement and decision of the person authorized to transact the business of the supervisor aforesaid, he may, within three months after such decision, appeal from the same, upon such items in the account as he shall specially designate, stating, in writing, his objection to the decision on the same, to the accounting officers of the treasury department; and, upon such appeal being taken and presented to the treasury department, within the time aforesaid, it shall be lawful for the accounting officers of that Department to audit and settle the same, according to the rules prescribed by this act, and in such manner as the justice of the case may require.

Sec. 3. *And be it further enacted,* That if upon the settlement of the accounts as aforesaid, of the said Conrad Laub, deceased, it shall appear that he is entitled to further credits than have heretofore been received, it shall be lawful for the Secretary of the Treasury to allow the same, and credit his account therewith.

Sec. 4 *And be it further enacted,* That, the legal and equitable allowance to be made, shall not exceed the balance which is due to the United States; nor shall any allowance, so ascertained, be passed to his credit, unless the administrator shall forthwith pay such remaining balance, if any, as shall, upon said settlement be found to be due and owing from the said Conrad Laub.

H. CLAY.
Speaker of the House of Representatives.
JOHN GAILLIARD,
President of the senate, pro tempore.
Washington, May 15, 1820.—Approved
JAMES MONROE.

An act to authorize the Governor of Illinois to obtain certain Abstracts of Lands from certain Public Officers.

Be it enacted by the senate and house of representatives of the United States of America in congress assembled, That it shall be the duty of the Register of the United States' land office at Vincenes in the state of Indiana to furnish to the Governor of the state of Illinois, when he shall apply for the same a complete abstract of all the lands which have been purchased at that office, or which may hereafter be purchased, which lie within the state of Illinois, designating the name of each purchaser, and the time of making the purchase; for which he shall be entitled to receive, from such applicant, at the rate of ten cents for each separate entry, a copy thereof is required: *Provided, however,* That all the expense incurred by virtue of this act, shall be defrayed by said state.

Sec. 2. *And be it further enacted,* That it shall be the duty of the Secretary of the Treasury, upon the application of the governor of said state, to cause a complete abstract to be made out, for the use of said state, of all the military bounty lands which have been patented to the soldiers of the late army, lying within the same designating the name of each patentee.

H. CLAY,
Speaker of the House of Representatives.
JOHN GAILLARD.
President of the senate pro tempore.
Washington, *May* 15, 1820.—Approved:
JAMES MONROE.

GEOGRAPHICAL DESCRIPTION OF FLORIDA.

Length 588.—Breadth, 228.—56,500 square miles.

Between 25 and 31 degrees of North latitude & 3 1-2 and 10 degrees 20 minutes West longitude.

Boundaries—On the north by Georgia and Alabama; on the south by the Gulf of Mexico; on the east by the Atlantic and Gulf of Florida, and on the West by the Gulf of Mexico, and part of Alabama.

Divisions—This country is divided into East Florida containing about 50,000 and West Florida about 6,500 square miles.

Population—The present population does not exceed 12,000, exclusive of Indians.—The inhabitants mostly reside in towns.

Chief Towns.—St. Augustine and Pensacola are the towns of much consideration.

St. Augustine, the capital of East Florida, is situated on the east coast, on the bay of St Augustine, in latitude 30 degrees north, and longitude 4 degrees 25 minutes west, containing 4000 inhabitants. It is a healthy place, having a high and dry situation, with the benefits of the sea breezes. The figure of the town is a parallelogram, laid out at the foot of an eminence on the beach, with four wide parallel streets, intersected by others of smaller dimensions, at right angles. The church of St. Augustine, with the monastery, are the most conspicuous edifices of the town. The town is well fortified; the castle St. Juan being built of stone, with four bastions, the curtains between which are 180 feet long and 20 feet high. The buildings are fire proof and partly case-mated. St. Augustine has resisted successfully several formidable attacks

Besides St. Augustine, there are several small villages in East Florida; the principal of which is St. Mark's situated on the river St. Mark's near Apalachia Bay.

Pensacola, the capital of West Florida is situated on the West side of Pensacola Bay having a fine harbor, safe from every wind, with plenty of water. Pensacola is in latitude 30 degrees 28 minutes north, and longitude 10 degrees west sixty miles east of Mobile. Its figure is a parallelogram one mile long, and a quarter of a mile wide; and it is accounted a healthy place. The entrance into the bay is fortified. The country north of the town is watered by the Escambia, Conecuch and Yellow rivers, rising in Alabama, and running into the Bay of Pensacola.

The other villages of West Florida are St. Joseph, near Cape St. Blaz, in the Gulf of Mexico; Wells, on the west side of St. Andrew's Bay; and Cambletown seven miles north-east of Pensacola, and at the head of the same bay.

Rivers.—Apalachicola, the principal river of the Floridas, rises at the point where North Carolina, South Carolina, Tennessee & Georgia approach; and running across the last, becomes the boundary for some distance, between it and Alabama. Leaving Alabama, it becomes the boundary between West Florida and Georgia, and at the mouth of Flint, flowing in from the north-east, it becomes the boundary of the two Floridas. It then proceeds towards the Gulf of Mexico, and discharges itself into St. George's sound, near Cape St. Blaz.

St. Mary's, rising in the Ekanufanoka swamp runs to the Atlantic between Georgia and East Florida.

St. John's, rises in the South of East Florida, & running north a short distance, forms Mayaca Lake. This lake throws out several small streams running east into the Atlantic, and south-west into the Gulf of Mexico; but the principal outlet proceeds directly north, forming in its way four other lakes, the chief of which is lake George. At Poppa, or Picolata, it changes its direction from north to east and runs into the Atlantic, near Talbot Island, about midway between St. Augustine and St. Mary's. The source, situation, course, length and outlet of this river, lead to a number of reflections in relation to the face of the country and its internal communications. In the first place, it would appear that lake Mayaca occupies the highest point of land in East Florida; streams running from it, by various directions, into the Atlantic and Gulf of Mexico In the second place, it has formed a water communication between the north-east and south-west shores of East Florida. In the third place, there is only sixty miles distance between Lake Geoge and Esperitu-Santa Bay, the rivers of the one interlocking with the waters of the other; making the communication by water from the Atlantic to the Gulf of Mexico very direct and short. In the fourth place, the river St. John's is a natural reservoir, to supply canals in every part of the territory, to shorten the conveyance of merchandize, between the Atlantic and the Gulf of Mexico. In the fifth place, a question is sugested, *whence came the springs that supply lake Mayaca?* It is higher than the level of the Atlantic and the Gulf of Mexico, as is proved by water falling in rapid currents from its basin into both. There are no lands on the Peninsula, higher than the lake itself, at least below the 30th degree of north latitude, which is distant from the lake 250 miles.

This sketch not being designed to discuss at length, physical questions arising out of the phenomena that appear on the face of the territory, more is not intended here, than barely to excite the investigation of naturalists and philosophers. It is deemed sufficient for the present, barely to intimate that lake Mayaca is supplied by a subterraneous channel, leading from a fountain situated in the upper regions of Georgia, perhaps in the Alleghany mountains. Calculating this covert channel of the St. John's it is perhaps the longest river running into the Atlantic.

Suhwanay, another river rising in the Ekaufanoka swamp, pursuing a winding course of 200 miles, falls in the Apalachia Bay. This is said to be the purest river in America, receiving in its course no tributary streams or creeks; but is supplied entirely by springs along its—banks. It is 200 yards wide, and twenty feet deep, at Talabo sochete in East Florida.

In addition to those already mentioned of East-Florida, there are running into the Atlantic. Naussa, India, Grenouille, St. Sebastian, St. Lucia, running into the Gulf of Mexico; North river, Haley's Amajura, running into Esperitu Santa Bay, Tampa, Hellsborough; Mannette; and running into the Apalachian Bay, St. Mark's and Oketockonne.

The rivers in West Florida are the Perdido, so called, because it loses itself under ground. Perdido Rio, signifying lost river, is the boundary between Mobile county in Alabama, and West Florida—Escambia, Connecah Yellow, St. Andrew's, Sweet water, &c.

Swamps.—The great Ekaufanoka, called by the natives, Ouaquaphenogau, lies between Georgia and East Florida, and is divided between them by an imaginary line. It is estimated at 302 miles in circumference, and in a wet season, has the appearance of a vast lake studded with islands. The soil of the islands, or firm land, in this immense morass, is indescribably rich, as is most of the marshy ground in both the Floridas. To clear, and put them into successful cultivation, will require immense labor.

Lakes.—The principal of these have already been mentioned in tracing the great river St John's of the south.

Islands.—Amelia, Talbot, St. Anastasia, Biscaino, Ball, Newcastle, Bradshaw, Tertugas, St. Georges, Corn Island, Roebuck, Santa Rosa.

Bays.—St. Augustine, Smyrna, Chatham, Charlotte, Esperitu Santa, St. Joseph, Apalachia, Pensacola, St. Andrews, Perdido, St. St. Mary's, Carlos Capes, Carneveral, Florida Sable, Roman, St. Biaz, &c.

Soil.—The major part is sandy, covered with long leaf pine. On the rivers, creeks, lakes and swamps, the soil is of the first quality, and produces sugar, cotton, corn, indigo, rice, etc. equal to the best lands in Georgia. Some of the islands are valuable on account of their fertility.

Produce.—In addition to those mentioned above, are potatoes, melons, ground peas, lemons, oranges, olives, figs, cocoa nuts, plumbs and cochineal.

Natural Growth.—Immense white and red oak, the splendid and beautiful magnolia, cypress, red and white oak, mulberry, hickory, sassafras, palms, walnuts, cabbage tree, &c. grow in masses, and form in summer the most delightful shades for man and beast. The flowering shrubbery and plants of Florida are indicated by the name of the country, and do not own their existence to fancy. Here the busy bee and the singing birds sport in ecstacies.

Animals.—Horses, flocks of sheep, goats, herds of cattle, and droves of swine, are reared in Florida. In desart places, wild animals, such as otters, hares, rabbits, racoons, foxes, opossums, squirrels, salamanders, gophers, alligators, & various reptiles abound. The alligators are frightfully large, but generally harmless; fewer accidents arising from their voracity or ferocity, notwithstanding their numbers, than from the viciousness of many of the domestic animals.

Government.—The Floridas, lately provinces of Spain, were under the captain-general of Havana, with military governors at St. Augustine and Pensacola, and commandants at the smaller posts. Since the treaty ceding them to the United States in 1812, congress passed an act, authorising the president to take possession in the event of the ratification of the treaty by the Spanish monarch, and to establish a provisional government for the territory.

Indians.—The Indians of Florida reside mostly in the neighborhood of Apalachia bay; but they are a vagrant people, wandering to and fro from the towns. They are called Seminoles, and as the name imports, are runaways from the Creeks and other nations to the north of Florida. Their habits are mean, little of the magnanimity of the Creeks, Cherokees, Choctaws, &c. remaining with them. Their vagabond habits have been encouraged by an association with the vilest swindlers and cut-throats—Americans, Englishmen & Spaniards—who have either fled from the justice of the laws, or resorted to this scheme for the sake of traffic with the Indians. This horrible band, augmented by runaway negroes, have been exceedingly troublesome to the peace and safety of the inhabitants of the south west counties of Georgia—steadily, robbing and murdering, until they were completely overthrown by General Jackson, in the short but vigorous campaign of 1818.

From the New-York American.

STATE OF EUROPE.

The very disturbed condition, as well of the continent as of the British isles, is far from consolatory to those who had anticipated a permanent settlement of the various conflicting interests of the nations of the old world. But the passions which the French revolution developed are neither to be allayed nor restrained by the conventional barriers, however skilfully erected, or vigilantly guarded, of theoretical statesmen. The truth it, that the whole ferment may be explained by the brief remark, that it arises from a struggle between the PEOPLE, who begin to know their rights and feel their power, and the monarchs and priviledged classes, who dessire to retain their ancient and hereditary ascendancy, and to exercise unquestioned sway over meaner men. Orators, statesmen, and even political writers still treat of the indefeasable rights of kings, and the nature and necessary privileges, exemptions, and immunities, as of nobles though the credulity of man on these subjects were yet unshaken; and however absurd, as it may appear to us here, they still seem to consider certain *casts born for dominion,* and the other more numerous classes for subjection. This is called the natural order of things, which it is equally treasonable to oppose or endeavor to subvert. It is fortuity, this blind and wayward adherence to ancient opinions and prejudices in rulers, that astonishes and perplexes us beyond measure. On this side of the Atlantic, it would appear to us about as reasonable to maintain that the sun revolves round the earth, or that the torrid zone is uninhabitable, or any other of the equally untenable propositions of the geography of past ages, as to reason gravely about the rights of any individeal, monarch or noble, to lord it over other men without their concurrence; and it would seem to us about as practicable to set bounds to the ocean, as to arrest the persevering march of the human mind on these subjects. The truth is, the impulse was long since given, and our own revolution as well as that of France, though in both instances hastened perhaps a little by the pressure of immediate and intolerable grievances, was the necessary result of the progress of intellectual light. This progress cannot be arrested: obstacles may indeed be cast in the way, and impediments multiplied, and the career thus rendered difficult and full of dangers, which otherwise would have been plain and harmless—but ultimately the triumph of knowledge is certain. Men will no longer submit to be at best the playthings, and too often the miserable victims of hereditary oppression. They will no longer consent to toil away their lives in poverty and suffering, at the bidding, and for the benefit, of imperious masters. They perceive that in all mental acquisitions, in all bodily accomplishments, they are equal to those before whom they have been accustomed to bow; and they cannot but ask themselves then, by what authority it has been decided that we and ours are for ever to remain in bondage, while others no whit superior to ourselves, are for ever to receive our homage? and when this question becomes habitual, there is an end of divine right and hereditary sway.

This we conceive to be the pressent condition of Europe. All classes are alive to their rights and intent upon asserting them: and it is the systematic and determined manner in which it appears to us, this process is going on throughout the great mass of the European population, that renders the opposition to it of monarchs or nobles, in our judgement, equally hopeless and impolitic. A free

FACING PAGE: ISSUE OF THE *HALCYON, AND TOMBECKBE PUBLIC ADVERTISER*, VOLUME 6, NO. 20, FROM SEPTEMBER 11, 1820. THERE IS A CONTEMPORARY NOTATION THAT THE ISSUE WAS FORWARDED TO THE SECRETARY OF STATE—QUITE LIKELY JOHN QUINCY ADAMS.

This weekly paper was established in St. Stephens, Alabama, in early 1815 by Thomas Eastin, Alabama's first state printer. Eastin, a veteran of the war of 1812, served as a quartermaster in Andrew Jackson's army. While the army was at Mount Vernon, Alabama, Eastin found a damaged printing press and purchased it. He removed the press to St. Stephens, Alabama, in time to publish a notice of the signing of the Treaty of Ghent. That treaty was signed in December of 1814 and ratified in February of 1815 after the battle of New Orleans had been fought and won by Jackson's troops. St. Stephens, located on the Tombigbee River above Mobile, was the territorial capital of Alabama from 1817 to 1819. The *Halcyon* was the fourth newspaper established in Alabama. With the removal of the state capital to Cahawba in 1819, St. Stephens began a gradual decline and had all but disappeared by the Civil War. It is today a historic site administered by the Old St. Stephens Historical Commission.

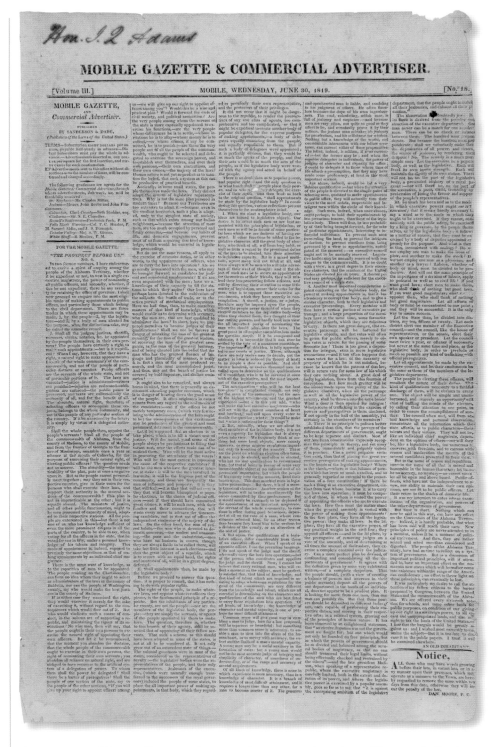

ISSUE OF THE *MOBILE GAZETTE & COMMERCIAL ADVERTISER*, VOLUME 3, NO. 19, FROM JUNE 30, 1819.

It is thought that this newspaper, founded in 1815 by G. B. Cotton, lasted for at least four years, shortening its name later to simply the *Gazette*. The *Gazette* was acquired in 1823 by the *Mobile Register*, which was founded in 1821. Copies of newspapers published during the period when Alabama was a territory are extremely rare, and this copy may be unique. There are indications that this issue was sent to the office of the US secretary of state, a contemporary hand has noted "Hon. J. Q. Adams" as the recipient. Adams was secretary of state from 1817 to 1825.

THE PLANTER'S ALMANAC FOR ALABAMA FOR 1837 AND 1841.

The Williams Collection holds one of the most significant groups of Alabama almanacs in institutional hands, ranging in date from 1831 to 1872 and including a number of Confederate almanacs.

These publications were vital to the planters of the state and persons engaged in farming of any type. The astronomical calculations were prepared for the meridian of Mobile but could be used for "the Adjoining states without material variation."

The 1837 almanac was published in Mobile by Woodruff, Fiske, and McGuire, and in Tuscaloosa by Woodruff, McGuire & Company. David Woodruff (1795–1876) was a prominent bookseller who came to Tuscaloosa from his native Connecticut in 1827 or 1828. In 1829 he married Antoinette Bell, who had previously come to Tuscaloosa to take charge of the Female Institute.

Their daughter, Virginia Hortense, married Confederate general Robert Emmett Rodes. Woodruff coproduced at least two Confederate publications. One was an 1863 almanac with calculations made at the University of Alabama and sold by Tuscaloosa and by a Macon bookseller. The other was delegate William R. Smith's history of the Alabama Secession Convention, published in 1861 and available from booksellers in Montgomery and Atlanta.

TITLE PAGE OF CICERO'S *ORATIONS*
(PHILADELPHIA: TOWAR AND HOGAN,
1828) OWNED BY JOSIAH GORGAS.

This edition, edited by John G. Smart, contained numerous notes from an earlier edition and a life of Cicero in English. Gorgas signed the book on the free end-paper.

Josiah Gorgas (1818–1883) was a native of Pennsylvania and a graduate of West Point in 1841. Promoted into the Ordnance Corps, Gorgas spent his entire military career in the field of artillery and explosives. Prior to and after service in the Mexican War, he served at almost every US arsenal in the country, including the arsenal at Mount Vernon, Alabama, between 1853 and 1856. It was during this tour of duty that he married Amelia Ross Gayle (1826–1913), daughter of Governor John Gayle.

With the outbreak of the Civil War Gorgas resigned from the US Army and returned to Alabama with his family. He was promoted to lieutenant colonel of artillery in the Confederate States Army in April of 1861. Assigned as chief of the Ordnance Bureau at that time, he held that position for the balance of the war, being promoted to brigadier general in November of 1864.

At the end of the war the family moved back to Alabama where Gorgas became superintendent of the Brierfield Iron Works. After a period as vice chancellor at the University of the South, General Gorgas accepted the presidency of the University of Alabama in 1878. The general's health began to fail in 1879, and the board of trustees reluctantly accepted his resignation, appointing him university librarian. In that capacity he was ably assisted by his wife until his retirement in 1882. At his death Amelia Gorgas was named university librarian and held that post until her retirement in 1906. A tireless worker for the university, she was a great favorite with the Corps of Cadets who called her "the angel of the campus."

Original binding of Gorgas's copy of Cicero's Orations.

Gorgas's signatures in his copy of Cicero's Orations.

M. T. CICERONIS

ORATIONES

QUÆDAM SELECTÆ,

IN

USUM DELPHINI,

CUM

INTERPRETATIONE ET HISTORIA SUCCINCTA

RERUM GESTARUM ET SCRIPTORUM

M. T. CICERONIS.

IN THIS EDITION ARE INTRODUCED ALL THE VALUABLE NOTES OF THE DAUPHIN
EDITION, TRANSLATED INTO ENGLISH, SELECTIONS FROM DUNCAN AND
OTHER COMMENTATORS, AND ORIGINAL OBSERVATIONS.

BY JOHN G. SMART.

SECOND EDITION, CORRECTED AND IMPROVED,

WITH A LIFE OF CICERO, IN ENGLISH.

Philadelphia:

PUBLISHED AND FOR SALE BY TOWAR AND HOGAN,
No. 255 Market Street.
••••
1828.

PRESIDENT ALVA WOODS'S
*BACCALAUREATE ADDRESS, PRESENTED
AUGUST 11, 1834, AT THE THIRD ANNUAL
COMMENCEMENT OF THE UNIVERSITY OF
THE STATE OF ALABAMA* (PUBLISHED BY
REQUEST OF THE TRUSTEES, 1834).

Alva W. Woods (1794–1887) was the first president of the University of Alabama and served in that capacity from April 12, 1831, to December of 1837. A native of Vermont, he was educated at Phillips Academy in Andover, Massachusetts, and Harvard University (then Harvard College). He graduated from there with honors in 1817. After four years of study at Andover Theological Seminary Woods was ordained a Baptist minister in 1821. He taught briefly at Columbian College (now George Washington University) and in 1824 was offered the position of professor of mathematics and natural philosophy at Brown University. Woods was appointed president of Transylvania University in Lexington, Kentucky, in 1828. A fire destroyed the main building of that institution in 1829 and so crippled the school for a time that Woods felt his services could be better utilized at another campus. When offered the presidency of the University of Alabama, he accepted.

His tenure at Tuscaloosa was apparently not a happy one for him or the university. Woods was opposed to slavery and had been recommended for the position by James G. Birney, a noted abolitionist. His relationship with the trustees, faculty, and student body must have suffered, as students openly rioted against his administration in July of 1837. Citing poor health and a desire to educate his son in a non–slave holding state were the reasons given for his resignation.

Woods moved his family to Providence, Rhode Island, to prepare his son to enter Brown University. He was a trustee of that institution from 1843 to 1859 and spent a great deal of his later years in philanthropic pursuits. For a number of years he traveled the state of Rhode Island, serving as chaplain to prisoners in various state institutions.

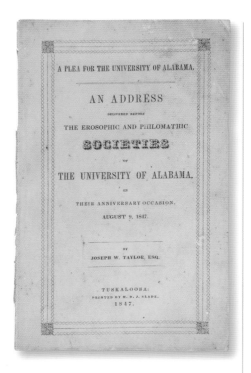

JOSEPH WATKINS TAYLOR'S *A PLEA
FOR THE UNIVERSITY OF ALABAMA:
AN ADDRESS PRESENTED BEFORE
THE EROSOPHIC AND PHILOMATHIC
SOCIETIES OF THE UNIVERSITY OF
ALABAMA, ON THEIR ANNIVERSARY
OCCASION, AUGUST 9, 1847*
(TUSKALOOSA: PRINTED BY M. D. J.
SLADE, 1847).

The University of Alabama officially opened its doors to students on April 18, 1831. The Erosophic Society was founded in May of that year, the Philomathic some eight months later. These two groups were primarily academic debate societies.

Joseph Watkins Taylor (1820–?) was a native of Kentucky and upon graduating from Cumberland College in 1838 moved to Alabama. He taught school in Greene County for two years and then commenced reading law in Eutaw, establishing a practice there. He was elected to the state legislature in 1845 and reelected in 1847. A strong supporter of public education and the university during his time in the state senate, he eventually became chairman of the senate committee on education. As did a number of Alabamians, he opposed secession but supported his adopted state in her decision. Elected to the US Congress in 1865, Taylor was not allowed to take his seat due to Republican Reconstruction policies. He was for a time involved with the editorship of the *Eutaw Whig* before moving to Tuscaloosa where he edited the *Times* newspaper.

Marmaduke Johnson Slade (1805–1857), the printer of the address, was a native of North Carolina. It is unclear when he moved to Tuscaloosa. He was editor and publisher of the weekly Tuscaloosa *Independent Monitor*.

FRONTISPIECE AND TITLE PAGE OF
THE FIRST EDITION OF JOSEPH G.
BALDWIN'S *THE FLUSH TIMES OF
ALABAMA AND MISSISSIPPI: A SERIES
OF SKETCHES* (NEW YORK: D.
APPLETON AND COMPANY, 1853).

Joseph Glover Baldwin (1815–1864) was born near Winchester, Virginia, and at an early age determined on a career in the legal profession. He studied law under his uncle Briscoe G. Baldwin, who would go on to serve in the Confederate army and secure a place on the staff of General Robert E. Lee. Deciding that one could make his fortune in a less settled place than Virginia, Baldwin moved to DeKalb, Mississippi, in 1836. The next eighteen years were spent in Mississippi and Alabama. The southwest frontier at this period was an unsettled and turbulent region, and Baldwin, who had come there to make his fortune, was both a participant in and keen observer of the situation. In 1839 he moved to Gainesville, Alabama, already noted for its wealth and culture. There he married Sidney White, daughter of Judge John White. Entering into state politics,

he experienced the pitfalls of that arena and in 1853 moved to Mobile. Baldwin entered a partnership with noted lawyer Phillip Phillips, but the lure of a new country led to his journeying to California in 1854. His legal career flourished, and he served as an associate justice of the state supreme court from 1858–1862.

The Flush Times of Alabama and Mississippi is an entertaining volume of Baldwin's impressions of these states during a period of relative political confusion and wild land

speculation, which resulted in a most litigious society. Baldwin had kept notes of his encounters with the unusual characters and scenes of the 1830s and 1840s. His shrewd observations, whether concerning the courtroom or barroom, as well as his perspective as a fortune seeker, allowed him to write perceptively and humorously about this period. In 1855 Baldwin published a volume entitled *Party Leaders*, giving a serious treatment to the careers of Jefferson, Hamilton, Clay, and others.

TITLE PAGE OF *REID'S TRAMP*
(SELMA: BOOK AND JOB OFFICE OF
JOHN HARDY & CO., 1858), JOHN
C. REID'S ACCOUNT OF HIS TRAVELS
THROUGH TEXAS, NEW MEXICO,
ARIZONA, AND CALIFORNIA.

Reid's journey commenced in Marion,
Alabama, in September of 1857 and ended
in the summer of 1858. While not an
important Alabama book as regards
its content, it is most desirable
as a rare Alabama imprint
as very few copies have
survived.

John Coleman Reid
(1824–1896) was a native
of Tuscaloosa County. Educated
at Memphis, Tennessee, he was admit-
ted to that state's bar in 1843. After practicing
in Tennessee for several years, he settled in
Marion, Alabama, circa 1851. In 1857 Reid,
at the head of the Messila Valley Company
began a ten-month exploration of the country
surrounding the Gadsden Purchase. He began
in earnest in Galveston, Texas, and ended
in California. Reid had been prominent in
Alabama politics before the Civil War and was
opposed to secession, but he followed the call
of his state into the Confederate army, rising
to the rank of colonel in the Twenty-eighth
Alabama Infantry. After the war he resumed
his law practice in Marion but moved his
practice to Selma in 1871.

Original
binding of
Reid's Tramp.

TITLE PAGE OF *WOODWARD'S REMINISCENCES OF THE CREEK, OR MUSCOGEE INDIANS, CONTAINED IN LETTERS TO FRIENDS IN GEORGIA AND ALABAMA* BY THOMAS S. WOODWARD (MONTGOMERY: BARRETT & WIMBISH, BOOK AND GENERAL JOB PRINTERS, 1859).

One of Rucker Agee's *Twenty Alabama Books* and one of the rarest of books relating to this region. This copy formerly belonged to a noted Alabama bibliophile and was the only copy he had been able to acquire in his collecting career. As that gentleman began dispersing his collection, he sold this copy to Steve Williams.

Thomas S. Woodward had a most unusual life. His date of birth in Georgia can only be assumed to have been in the 1790s. He enlisted as a private in the War of 1812 and fought in the Creek War in 1813–1814. Woodward quickly won the friendship of Andrew Jackson who fostered Woodward's rapid rise in Jackson's frontier command. Jackson sent him to Florida in 1817 to deal with some problems arising with the Seminole Indians. Woodward was commissioned a brigadier general in the Alabama Brigade in 1820. He served as an escort to the Marquis de Lafayette during his visit to Alabama in 1824 and saw service in the state during the Second Creek War in 1836.

One of the founders of Tuskegee, Woodward later moved to southern Arkansas and eventually to north-central Louisiana. He founded the town of Montgomery, Louisiana, dying there on December 24, 1859. His reminiscences were originally published as a series of letters in the *Montgomery (AL) Mail* in 1857 and 1858. Woodward's intimate contacts with the Native Americans in the region make this an important source for the study of the relationship between the two cultures during this period.

WOODWARD'S REMINISCENCES

OF THE

Creek, or Muscogee Indians,

Contained in Letters to Friends in

GEORGIA AND ALABAMA.

BY THOMAS S. WOODWARD, OF LOUISIANA,
(FORMERLY OF ALABAMA.)

WITH AN APPENDIX.
CONTAINING INTERESTING MATTER RELATING TO THE GENERAL SUBJECT.

MONTGOMERY, ALA.:
BARRETT & WIMBISH, BOOK AND GENERAL JOB PRINTERS.
1859.

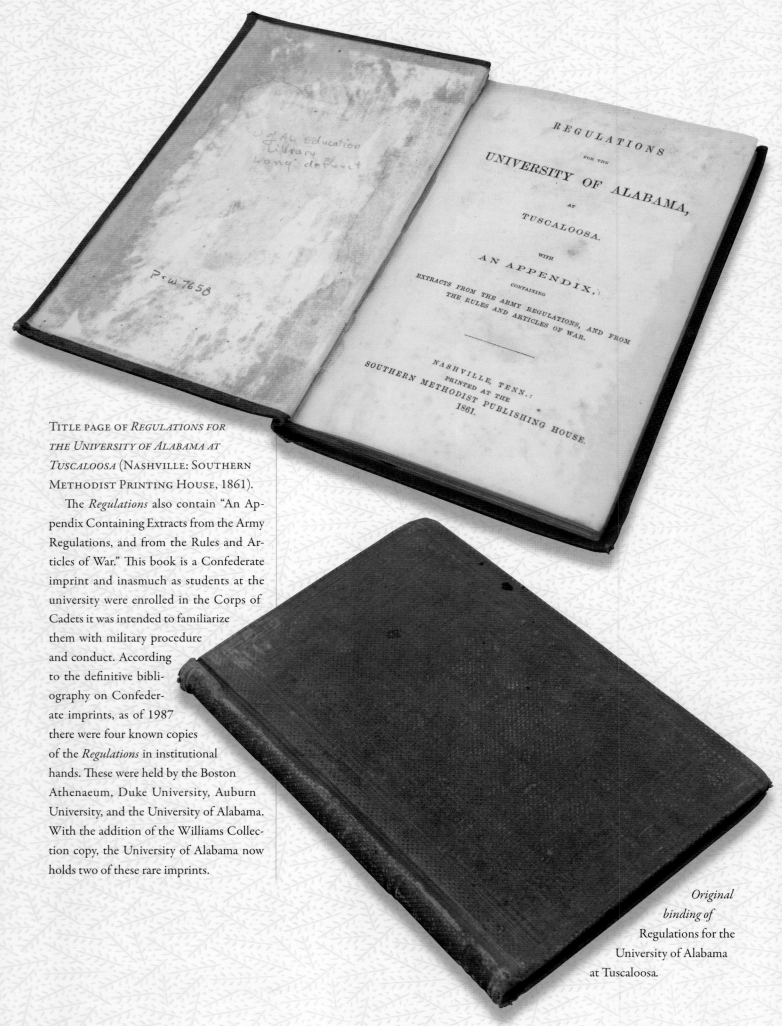

Title page of *Regulations for the University of Alabama at Tuscaloosa* (Nashville: Southern Methodist Printing House, 1861).

The *Regulations* also contain "An Appendix Containing Extracts from the Army Regulations, and from the Rules and Articles of War." This book is a Confederate imprint and inasmuch as students at the university were enrolled in the Corps of Cadets it was intended to familiarize them with military procedure and conduct. According to the definitive bibliography on Confederate imprints, as of 1987 there were four known copies of the *Regulations* in institutional hands. These were held by the Boston Athenaeum, Duke University, Auburn University, and the University of Alabama. With the addition of the Williams Collection copy, the University of Alabama now holds two of these rare imprints.

Original binding of Regulations for the University of Alabama at Tuscaloosa.

FRONT WRAP OF *ACTS OF THE LEGISLATURE AND BY-LAWS FOR THE ERECTION, ORGANIZATION AND GOVERNMENT OF THE ALABAMA INSANE HOSPITAL AT TUSCALOOSA* (TUSCALOOSA: PRINTED AT THE "OBSERVER" BOOK AND JOB OFFICE, 1861).

This thirty-two page pamphlet provided legislative history along with governing rules and was issued prior to the opening of the hospital. This publication is called a Confederate imprint, meaning it appeared in print after Alabama joined the Confederacy and before the end of the Civil War. Many of these publications are quite rare, and there are only two known copies of this imprint in institutional collections. With the acquisition of the Williams copy the University of Alabama now owns both.

Plans for a state hospital for the mentally ill began in 1852 and were organized along the progressive concepts advocated by Dorothea Dix and Thomas Story Kirkbride. The building, begun in 1853 and designed by noted architect Samuel Sloan, was completed in 1859. Its layout was modeled on the hospital plan originated by Kirkbride and was the first building in Tuscaloosa with gas lighting and central heat. The first superintendent was Dr. Peter Bryce (1834–1892), a native of South Carolina, who was brought to the attention of the trustees by Dorothea

Dix. Under Bryce's "moral treatment plan" the use of shackles and other forms of restraint was discouraged and the patients were encouraged to work at familiar tasks. An attempt was made to allow the patients to lead as normal a life as possible while in treatment. The hospital was later renamed Bryce Hospital, and the building was added to the National Register of Historic Places in 1977.

BELOW: AN 1862 RECEIPT FOR A DOUBLE-BARREL SHOTGUN PURCHASED BY THE STATE OF ALABAMA.

With the outbreak of the Civil War weapons of all types were in short supply in the South. Alabama attempted to alleviate this by purchasing privately held weapons, mostly shotguns and fowling pieces. This gun was to be delivered to the quartermaster of "the University at Tuscaloosa" at which time Jefferson Isbell of Walker County was to receive a payment of twenty dollars.

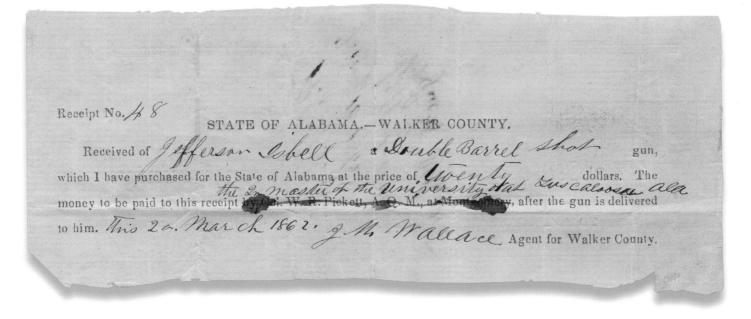

that town on February 6, crossing the Alabama state line that day, and spending the night in Cuba. Bates reached Montgomery on February 16, and in his account entitled *The Triumphal March of Sergeant Bates from Vicksburg to Washington*, published in 1868, he states the following: "I reached Montgomery on the 16th of February. Here I met with a magnificent reception. The ladies of this city made for me a beautiful pink sash, of fine silk, and ornamented with heavy gold fringe. It was presented to me at a public festival given to aid some charitable purpose, and is really a very beautiful sash." Bates is shown wearing the sash in the signed carte de visite pictured, taken in Columbia, South Carolina. Bates passed through Columbus, Macon, Milledgeville, and Augusta, Georgia, then through Columbia and Chester, South Carolina. He stopped in Charlotte, Greensboro, and Raleigh, North Carolina. After passing through Danville, Richmond, and Alexandria, Virginia, he arrived in Washington on April 14, 1868. The sergeant had been allowed to fly the flag over a number of public buildings, including the state capitol in Richmond, but in an ironic twist he was not allowed to fly it over the US Capitol. Angered at this insult, Bates unfurled it at the Washington Monument.

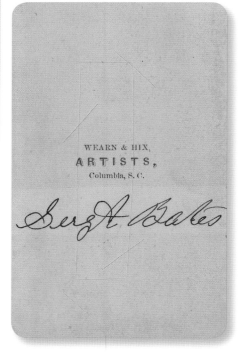

CARTE DE VISITE OF GILBERT H. BATES.
Gilbert H. Bates (1836–1917) was a native of Wisconsin and a farmer before the Civil War. Bates served as a sergeant in the First Wisconsin Heavy Artillery, returning to his farm near Albion, Wisconsin, at the end of the war. In November of 1867 Bates was conversing with a neighbor who claimed that the Southern people were still disloyal rebels and that the US flag was disrespected among them except in the presence of federal troops.

Bates demurred and proposed to carry the flag from the Mississippi River through the former Confederacy alone, unarmed, and without any money. A bet was wagered that if Bates were successful, the neighbor would pay him the sum of one dollar a day for each day of the trek.

Bates left Vicksburg, Mississippi, on January 28, 1868, after receiving a royal welcome in that city. He proceeded through Jackson and Meridian, Mississippi, leaving

Broadside sale inventory of items belonging to Peter Alexander Greene of Seale, Alabama, circa 1903–1906. The sale was managed by his kinsman, Peter Alexander Brannon, who was a practicing pharmacist in Columbus, Georgia, at the time.

Peter Alexander Greene (1838–1902) was born in Georgia, and after being educated by his parents and in the local schools, he began teaching at the age of eighteen. After attending Emory and Henry College and the East Alabama Male College at Auburn, he left school to join the Confederate army. Greene transferred from the Sixth Alabama Infantry to the Thirty-first Georgia Infantry in 1862 and was promoted to first lieutenant the following year. He was captured with his command during the retreat to Appomattox in 1865.

He was a planter from 1867 to 1880, at which time he was elected circuit court clerk of Russell County, holding that office until his death. Greene began his collecting activities in earnest at that time, although he had long held an avid interest in such matters. At his death his collection contained "about 3,000 stone aboriginal (native American) relics, some fifty or more fire-arms, twenty-five swords and a large assortment of old books, manuscripts, newspapers, curios, etc.," according to Alabama historian Thomas M. Owen. Interesting items listed in this sale under the heading Civil War Relics include "buttons from the vest of General R.E. Lee" and "one large lot of correspondence" relating to the objections by various Creek Indian chiefs to preaching in their nation by Methodist ministers, covering the period from 1821 to 1825.

Peter Alexander Brannon (1882–1967) was born in Seale and educated in the public schools there. He attended Alabama Polytechnic Institute (now Auburn University) from 1898 to 1900 and was awarded a degree in pharmacy. From 1900 to 1911 he practiced his vocation variously in Talladega, Troy, and Montgomery, Alabama, and in Co-

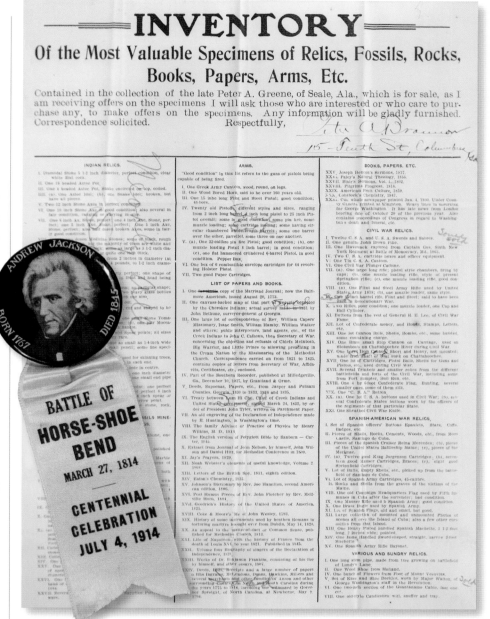

INSET: *Badge relating to the centennial celebration of the Battle of Horseshoe Bend in 1914 from the Brannon badge group.*

lumbus, Georgia. His long association with the Alabama Department of Archives and History (ADAH) began in 1911 and lasted until his death in 1967. Quickly promoted to chief clerk he became curator in 1920, holding that position until being named the third director in 1955.

A prolific writer, Brannon contributed articles to various publications on virtually all facets of Alabama and local history. His interest in fossils and Native American tribes led to an intensive study of the Creek Nation. Brannon was a prominent figure in the activities of the Alabama Anthropological Society (AAS).

The Williams Collection contains a number of items that once belonged to Brannon, including his pharmacy diploma, several photographic archives relating to the AAS, and an important collection of political badges. Also of note is his collection of badges and ribbons relating to the activities of the United Confederate Veterans and related organizations in Alabama. A significant Alabama historical autograph collection gathered by Brannon also forms part of the collection.

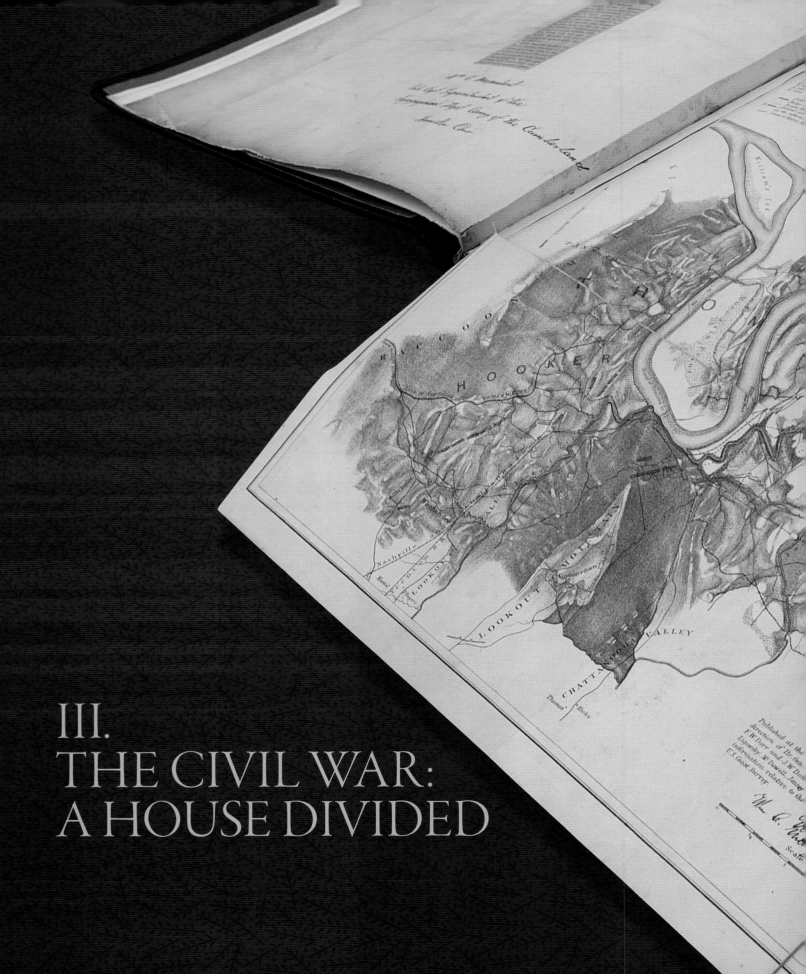

III.
THE CIVIL WAR: A HOUSE DIVIDED

Battlefield of
CHATTANOOGA
with the operations of the National Forces
under the command of
MAJ. GEN. U. S. GRANT
during the battles of Nov. 23·24 & 25 1863.

BATTLEFIELD OF
CHATTANOOGA WITH THE
OPERATIONS OF THE NATIONAL
FORCES UNDER THE COMMAND
OF MAJ. GEN. U. S. GRANT DURING
THE BATTLES OF NOV. 23, 24, & 25, 1863.

This beautifully lithographed and colored map was produced by the US Coast Survey Office from information compiled under the direction of Brigadier-General William F. Smith. Smith was Ulysses S. Grant's chief engineer during this campaign and his field surveys were forwarded to Washington, DC, to produce highly detailed maps. Smith was rewarded with a significant command under Grant in the operations in Virginia in the spring of 1864 but was later relieved after a quarrel with General Benjamin Butler, his direct superior. A later issue of this map was produced by the New York Lithographers' Association for the benefit of the US Sanitary Commission. Sales of this map were used to raise funds for the care of sick or wounded Union soldiers and their dependent families. The album, compiled by Captain William C. Margedant of the Topographical Engineering Department of the Army of the Cumberland, features a wealth of materials relating to the battles waged in the Chattanooga area. This was Captain Margedant's personal copy and bears his signature.

STEVE WILLIAMS'S INTEREST in American history led him to assemble what is assuredly one of the finest, if not the finest, collections on the Civil War. The book collection is perhaps unique in that Williams collected on all aspects of the Confederate experience, from military memoirs and unit histories to civilian accounts and other primary sources. All theaters of conflict are represented, as well as naval operations, social and economic history, and the era of Reconstruction. An important part of the collection relates to Confederate imprints—materials printed in the South during the period 1861 to 1865. Period and postbellum maps provide an insight into the cartographic skills of wartime engineers, an album assembled by Captain William Margedant of the Union engineer corps, for example, was a significant addition to the collection, containing copies of his maps and photographs. The Civil War was, of course, the first major conflict to be extensively photographed. The Williams collection is replete with battlefield stereographs and cartes de visite, as well as larger formats. Included are a number of original albumin photographs by George N. Barnard, and the centerpiece of this group: a copy of *Gardner's Photographic Sketch Book of the War*, presented to the Union general Phillip H. Sheridan by Northern spymaster Allan Pinkerton. Additionally, there are hundreds of carte de visite–style images of Confederate and Union officers, public officials, and prominent civilians, a number of them signed. As previously mentioned, the group of Confederate imprints assembled by Williams is a most significant part of the collection. Numbering over 450 carefully selected items, with 45 previously unrecorded, it places the University of Alabama Libraries into an elite class in this genre. The collection also contains numerous rare prints and engravings of the principal actors and events of the war. As an important adjunct to the primary and scholarly history of the war from the Southern perspective, there is an exceptionally fine collection of books relating to the Union side of the conflict, paralleling, but to a lesser extent, the themes of the Confederate collection.

ALBUM CONTAINING ORIGINAL PHOTOGRAPHS, MAPS, AND DRAWINGS COMPILED BY CAPTAIN WILLIAM C. MARGEDANT OF THE TOPOGRAPHICAL ENGINEERING DEPARTMENT OF THE ARMY OF THE CUMBERLAND.

This personal archive of Captain Margedant contains more than one hundred pages of large format and carte de visite format photographs, maps, and original drawings done during the Civil War. Included is extensive photographic coverage of the Chattanooga area, showing scenes of the war and the destruction resulting from the conflict. There are also examples of military maps made by Margedant utilizing a process he developed.

Chemically treated paper was placed under the original tracing paper, on which a map was drawn in heavy black ink. Exposed to sunlight the blank areas of the paper became darkened. The ink on the original tracing blocked the sunlight, leaving the treated paper white beneath it. The resulting blue maps had white rivers and roads, which were differently colored to avoid confusion. Reproductions could be made quickly from the original and distributed to units in the field.

Captain Margedant, a resident of Hamilton, Ohio, enlisted at the outbreak of the war. After brief field service in western Virginia, his talents as a topographical engineer resulted in his being assigned in that capacity in May 1863 to the Army of the Cumberland, then commanded by Willam S. Rosecrans. In March of 1864 he was promoted to superintendent of the topographical engineering department. Margedant served with the army until June of 1864 when his old regiment, the Tenth Ohio Infantry, was discharged. At the request of General George H. Thomas he volunteered (without pay) to stay with the army until the end of July.

Original binding of the Margedant album.

ABOVE: *Photograph of the steamer* Kingston *at a landing near Chattanooga from the Margedant album.*

ABOVE: *Field-produced copy of a military map from the Margedant album.* RIGHT: *An original pen and ink drawing of the Battle above the Clouds, November 24, 1863, one of several engagements resulting in the raising of the Confederate siege of Chattanooga, Tennessee.*

COLONEL

CAPTAIN
INFANTRY
APPROVED BY WAR DEPARTMENT

FIRST LIEUTENANT

LTH. OF HOYER & LUDWIG RICHMOND

LITH. OF B. DUNCAN. CO

ABOVE: *Color plate from* Uniform and Dress *illustrating artillery uniforms for a sergeant, a private, and a musician.* RIGHT: *Color plate from* Uniform and Dress *illustrating infantry uniforms for a colonel, a captain, and a first lieutenant.*

THE WILLIAMS COLLECTION IS
REMARKABLE IN HAVING ALL THREE
EDITIONS OF THE RARE *UNIFORM
AND DRESS OF THE ARMY OF THE
CONFEDERATE STATES*.

The first was printed without plates in
Richmond, Virginia, in 1861 by Charles H.
Wynne and measured eighteen centimeters
high. That same year Wynne produced two
other editions (some authorities assign
a possible appearance date of early
1862), each with fifteen plates. One
edition was issued with colored lithographic plates, the other without color.
The size of the volumes was also changed,
these later editions measuring almost
thirty-six centimeters.

LEFT: *Title page from the 1861 edition of*
Uniform and Dress *illustrated with color
lithographs.* BELOW: *Original bindings of
the two later editions of* Uniform and Dress,
which contained the lithographic plates.

TO THE TRADE.

The undersigned have in hand a Southern edition of WEBSTER'S ELEMENTARY SPELLING BOOK—which will be an exact reprint of the Northern edition. It will be out about the *first of January*, and as the edition will be limited, we respectfully suggest that you order *at once* the quantity you will need. Persons ordering 50 dozen and upwards will be entitled to have their *imprint* on all they buy. Owing to the high price of paper and binding materials, the price to the trade will be $3.00 per dozen. A discount of 10 per cent will be allowed to parties purchasing 50 dozen and upwards. Address

BURKE, BOYKIN & CO.

Macon Ga., October 21st, 1862.

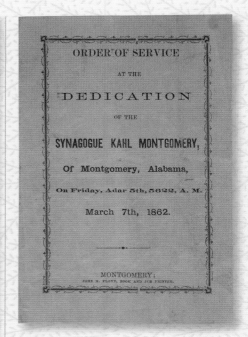

ORDER OF SERVICE AT THE DEDICATION OF THE SYNAGOGUE KAHL MONTGOMERY, Of Montgomery, Alabama, On Friday, Adar 5th, 5622, A. M. March 7th, 1862.

MONTGOMERY: JOHN M. FLOYD, BOOK AND JOB PRINTER.

A PREVIOUSLY UNRECORDED CONFEDERATE IMPRINT CELEBRATING THE DEDICATION OF SYNAGOGUE KAHL MONTGOMERY, BELIEVED TO BE THE ONLY SYNAGOGUE BUILT IN THE SOUTH DURING THE CIVIL WAR.

The synagogue's roots date to 1849 with the formation of Kahl Montgomery, the city's first formal Jewish congregation. A bequest from Jewish philanthropist Judah Touro of New Orleans enabled the congregation to erect the synagogue. The congregation aligned itself in 1874 with the Reform movement of Judaism, and the synagogue was renamed Temple Beth Or.

AN UNRECORDED 1862 CONFEDERATE IMPRINT PROSPECTUS ISSUED BY MACON, GEORGIA, BOOKSELLERS BURKE, BOYKIN AND COMPANY.

The prospectus announces a Southern edition of Webster's *Elementary Spelling Book*. Burke, Boykin and Company did publish this speller in three editions, the first in 1863 running to 156 pages. There are three known copies of that edition, one at Emory University, one at the Virginia State Library, and one at the Alabama Department of Archives and History. This firm issued a Second Southern Edition in 1863, known only in one incomplete copy, and a Third Southern Edition in 1865. Yale University, the Boston Athenaeum, and Emory University possess copies of that edition. The Williams Collection contains forty-five imprints of which it holds the only known institutional copy.

The original envelope that accompanied the Burke, Boykin and Company prospectus for Webster's Elementary Spelling Book.

CARTE DE VISITE OF COLONEL
BARRINGTON S. KING AND HIS
TWO-VOLUME SET OF CONFEDERATE
COLONEL (LATER LIEUTENANT
GENERAL) WILLIAM J. HARDEE'S *RIFLE
AND INFANTRY TACTICS, REVISED AND
IMPROVED BY COLONEL W. J. HARDEE*
(MOBILE: S. H. GOETZEL, 1861).

The only true copyright editions
were published by the Mobile printing firm of Sigmund H. Goetzel
over the first three years of the
war, covering nine editions.
Goetzel, a native of Austria,
arrived in Mobile in 1854
to open a bookstore.
By 1857 he had en-
tered the printing and
publishing business, and his
major antebellum book was Madame
Octavia Walton Le Vert's *Souvenirs of Travel*,
one of five titles issued that year. Goetzel's
wartime publications included British colonel A. J. L. Fremantle's *Three Months in the
Confederate States: April, June, 1863*; Sally
Rochester Ford's *Raids and Romance of Morgan and His Men;* and a Confederate edition
of Charles Dickens's *Great Expectations*.
Goetzel published nothing after 1865, and
his antebellum career is clouded in mystery.

Barrington S. King (1833–1865) was
a native of Liberty County, Georgia, and
before the war he was a physician in Columbia, South Carolina. Enlisting as a private
in Company C of the cavalry battalion of
Cobb's Georgia Legion, he was promoted
to captain in 1862. While commanding
C Company (the "Roswell Troopers"), he
purchased these copies of Hardee's *Rifle
and Infantry Tactics*. The photograph, which
shows him as lieutenant colonel of the
Cobb's Legion cavalry battalion was taken by
the Richmond studio of Charles R. Rees &
Co. After transferring to the Ninth Georgia
Cavalry in 1865, King was killed in action
near Averasboro, North Carolina.

William Joseph Hardee (1815–1873) was
an 1838 West Point graduate and served in
the US Army for the next twenty-three years,

rising to the rank of
lieutenant colonel. In
1853–1854 Hardee began
a project to rewrite the army's
primary drill manual *Rifle and Light Infantry
Tactics*. Completed in 1855, its acceptance
assured his position in the prewar army.
An assignment as commandant of cadets at
West Point followed and lasted from 1856
to 1860. His Confederate career saw his
promotion to lieutenant general in 1862,
and from then until the summer of 1864 he
commanded a corps in the Army of Tennessee. Disagreeing with the tactics employed
by General John B. Hood, Hardee asked for
and received a transfer, ending the war with
a command in North Carolina. Hardee and
his family returned to Alabama after the war
where he managed property belonging to his
second wife. He moved to Selma, Alabama,
in 1866, and there he engaged in several
business enterprises until his death.

MEMORIAL TO THE CONFEDERATE
CONGRESS FROM GENERAL WILLIAM
J. HARDEE AND S. H. GOETZEL
REQUESTING THAT BODY GRANT
HARDEE A SPECIAL COPYRIGHT FOR
HIS EDITION OF HARDEE'S *TACTICS*
THAT WOULD ESTABLISH HIS RIGHTS
AS A CONFEDERATE CITIZEN.

Hardee's existing contract was with
the Philadelphia firm of J. B. Lippincott,
dating from 1855, but Lippincott, due to
circumstances at the time, did not copyright
the work. This memorial was an attempt by
Hardee to protect his copyright.

BELOW: BINDING AND TITLE PAGE OF THE CONFEDERATE IMPRINT VERSION OF ADMIRAL RAPHAEL SEMMES'S *THE CRUISE OF THE ALABAMA AND THE SUMTER. FROM THE PRIVATE JOURNALS AND OTHER PAPERS OF COMMANDER R. SEMMES, C.S.N., AND OTHER* OFFICERS (LONDON: SAUNDERS, OTLEY & CO.; RICHMOND: WEST & JOHNSON, 1864).

The book was printed in London, and it is assumed that copies of this work ran the blockade into the South, which may account for its significant rarity. Prior to the University of Alabama acquiring the Williams Collection there were only four copies in institutional libraries, none of which were in Alabama.

LEFT: THE ONLY KNOWN CONFEDERATE IMPRINT OF AN ALABAMA LEGISLATIVE ACT DESIGNED TO AID THE FAMILIES OF INDIGENT CONFEDERATE SOLDIERS.

Entitled "An Act to Contibute to the Support of Indigent Families of Soldiers in the Military Service from the State of Alabama," the bill was signed by T. H. Watts, governor of Alabama, on December 8, 1863, and appropriated three million dollars to support eligible families. The legislature of Alabama appropriated money for this cause again in 1864, which is indicative of the deep concern for these families by their fellow Alabamaians.

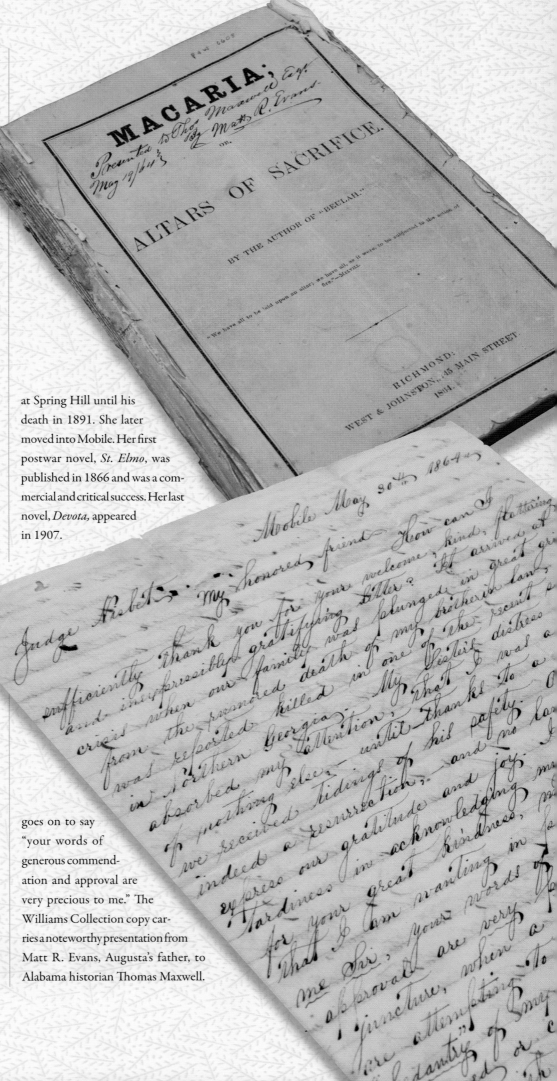

Front wrapper of Augusta Jane Evans's novel *Macaria; Or, Altars of Sacrifice* (Richmond: West & Johnston, 1864).

Augusta Jane Evans Wilson (1835–1909) was a prolific author whose novel *Macaria* was one of the most, if not the most, popular novels written in the Confederacy. Evans was born in Columbus, Georgia, and had published two other novels before the war. Her second, *Beulah,* appeared in 1859 to a certain amount of critical acclaim. *Macaria* is at best a somewhat turgid romance, full of classical allusions that some critics decried, saying that she was writing on a plane well above her intended audience. The books popularity was evident in both the Union and Confederacy. Federal soldiers read it avidly, and its importation into areas controlled by the Union was in some cases forbidden.

Evans established a private hospital in Mobile during the war and raised money for various Confederate causes. A military camp near Mobile was named Camp Beulah in her honor. In 1868 she married Lorenzo Madison Wilson and lived with him at his home at Spring Hill until his death in 1891. She later moved into Mobile. Her first postwar novel, *St. Elmo,* was published in 1866 and was a commercial and critical success. Her last novel, *Devota,* appeared in 1907.

Letter from Augusta Jane Evans to Judge Eugenius Aristides Nisbet, dated May 30, 1864, from Mobile.

In this letter to her friend Evans notes that there have been some brief notices of *Macaria* in which "the objection is urged by some, that 'the book is too learned,' ... I would simply remind my perplexed critics, of the pithy reply of Dr. Johnson, when some one found great fault with his dictionary: 'Sir! I am bound to furnish good definitions, but not brains to comprehend them.'" Judge Eugenius Aristides Nisbet (1803–1871), a Georgia legislator and state supreme court judge, had obviously written a most complimentary letter about the book. In her letter she goes on to say "your words of generous commendation and approval are very precious to me." The Williams Collection copy carries a noteworthy presentation from Matt R. Evans, Augusta's father, to Alabama historian Thomas Maxwell.

The wallpaper-backed front also has the title page information with a printed border. The copy shown here is the second edition; the first printing was in 1863, and both had wallpaper wraps. The use of wallpaper is almost exclusively confined to imprints issued by Goetzel although two other publishers, in Raleigh, North Carolina, and Richmond, Virginia, issued at least one title with wallpaper wraps. It has been a subject of debate whether the use by Goetzel was for paper conservation or decorative purposes or both.

Sally Rochester Ford (1828–1902) was born in Boyle County, Kentucky. A prewar novelist, her books included *Grace Truman, or, Love and Principle* (1857) and *Mary Bunyan, The Dreamer's Blind Daughter: A Tale of Religious Persecution* (1860). Ford published at least two more novels after the war. *Raids and Romance* proved to be one of the more popular Confederate novels. A Southern reviewer in 1863 declared: "It is written in a fascinating style, combining with its historical accuracy the exciting interest of a first class romance."

Above: Front and rear wraps of an 1864 Confederate almanac published by Burke, Boykin and Company of Macon, Georgia, and sold by B. B. Davis in Montgomery, Alabama.

As noted on the front wrap, the calculations were made at the University of Alabama. The back wrap contains an advertisement for Mobile bookseller H. C. Clarke and a request for buying rags to be used in paper manufacturing by Burke, Boykin and Company. The Williams Collection has the only copy in institutional hands.

Benjamin Bullock Davis (1829–1888) was born in Philadelphia, Pennsylvania, and trained for the drug business in that city. He moved to Montgomery in 1850 and was associated with the firm of Coxe and Hutchings, and later formed a hardware business also in Montgomery. Davis had a brief career as a bookseller and worked in Montevallo for a period during the war. Returning to Montgomery after the war, he formed a new hardware concern with a Mr. Ware and in 1877 bought out his partner and removed the business to Eufaula, Alabama. Davis died in Philadelphia while visiting his sister.

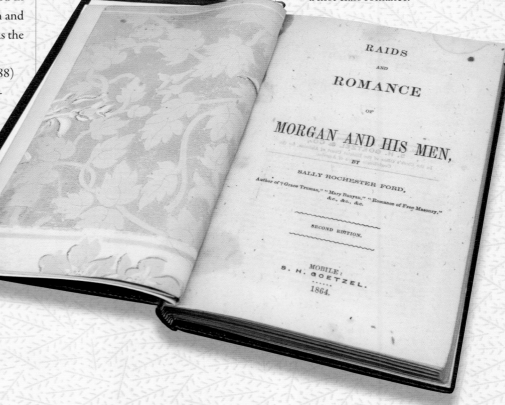

Front wrap of Colonel Arthur James Lyon Fremantle's account of his journey through the Confederacy in the summer of 1863, *Three Months in the Confederate States* (Mobile: S. H. Goetzel, 1864).

Originally published in Edinburgh in 1863, this Confederate imprint was an authorized edition by Goetzel of Mobile, printed in 1864. It has the wallpaper front and back wrap favored by that firm for a number of its publications.

Sir Arthur James Lyon Fremantle (1835–1901) was a young lieutenant colonel of the illustrious Coldstream Guards assigned to the post of Gibraltar in 1862. There a chance meeting with Confederate naval captain Raphael Semmes confirmed his interest in seeing the Southern side of the

war. His *Three Months in the Confederate States* covers his experiences during the period from April to June 1863

Entering the Confederacy through Texas in April of 1863, he traveled to the Army of Tennessee via Jackson, Mississippi, Mobile, and Atlanta, meeting generals Bragg and Beauregard. Joining Robert E. Lee's army just prior to the campaign into Pennsylvania, Fremantle observed the Battle of Gettysburg from his position as a "guest" on General James Longstreet's staff. Fremantle had a long and distinguished career in the British army, rising to the rank of major general and to the command of the Brigade of Guards during a portion of the Sudan expedition in 1884.

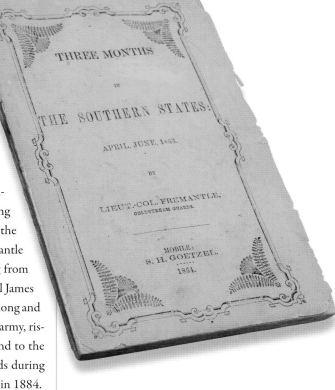

Three images taken by the firm of McPherson and Oliver after the fall of Fort Morgan, Alabama, in 1864.

William D. Pherson was born in Boston, Massachusetts in 1833. He worked in Boston during the period 1856–1861 and was listed as a photographer in Concord, New Hampshire, in 1862.

The photographic partnership of William D. McPherson and Mr. Oliver (no first name seems to be available) visited a number of sites in the Louisiana-Alabama theatre of

war. The firm produced a group of photographs of the Confederate bastion at Port Hudson, Louisiana, after its fall in July 1863, as well as a number of views of Baton Rouge, Louisiana. They traveled in early 1864 with the Union forces in the abortive Red River Campaign in which the North failed to capture Shreveport, Louisiana.

After the capture of Fort Morgan, Alabama, in August of 1864 McPherson and Oliver extensively photographed that installation, copyrighting twenty-three separate views on October 1, 1864. Copies of their

photographs were appended to the official report of the US Army Engineers on that campaign as some of their images had been to the official report of the siege of Port Hudson.

The firm established itself in New Orleans in 1864 at 133 Canal Street and became noted for a number of fine outdoor city photographs, especially in the Vieux Carre. The partnership was dissolved in 1865, and McPherson worked alone at 132 Canal until his death in 1867 from yellow fever.

This monumental two-volume work was published in two editions in Washington, DC, in 1865 and 1866 by Philp & Solomons. It contains one hundred photographic plates and sold for $150 on publication. There were one hundred copies of each edition. According to a census assembled by Gardner's biographer, there are fewer than twenty complete sets of the two hundred published, the other sets having been broken up and sold as individual plates. The Williams Collection copy, which includes both volumes, is from the second edition of 1866 but has the distinction of having been owned by Lieutenant General Philip Henry Sheridan. It was presented to him in 1869 by famed Union secret agent Allan Pinkerton.

Alexander Gardner (1821–1882) was born in Paisley, Scotland. Apprenticed as a silversmith jeweler at fourteen, by the age of thirty he was owner and editor of the *Glasgow Sentinel* newspaper. London in 1851 was the scene of a major exhibition at the famed Crystal Palace. The theme was "Industry of All Nations," and the exhibits including printing and book-binding arts, jewelry manufacture, and new developments in various scientific instruments. Photography held a prominent place, and American Matthew Brady won the grand prize for daguerrotypes. It is thought that Gardner's interest in photography began when he attended this exhibition.

Gardner and his family moved to America in 1856. He had practiced photography on a limited scale in Scotland in 1855 and 1856 and upon arriving in New York initiated contact with Matthew Brady. Gardner worked with Brady from 1856 to 1861 and was manager of his Washington gallery at the outbreak of the war. Gardner maintained a mutually beneficial relationship with Brady and his studio during the war. However, the fact remains that Gardner and others, notably George N. Barnard, James F. Gibson, and Timothy O'Sullivan, took most of the photographs in the field. After the end of the war, Gardner was the only photographer allowed to photograph the hanging of the group convicted of conspiring to murder Abraham Lincoln.

Perhaps the most famous view in Gardner's Sketch Book, volume 1, plate 23, is entitled President Lincoln on Battle-Field of Antietam. *This image was taken by Alexander Gardner in October 1862. It shows Lincoln towering over General George B. McClellan, whom he was soon to replace as commander of the Union Army of the Potomac. McClellan is the short man on the left in the foreground (there are three figures between Lincoln and the general).*

This print from Gardner's Sketch Book, *volume 1, plate 18, is entitled* Ruins of the Norfolk Navy Yard, Virginia. *The mount identifies the photographer as Gardner's brother, James.*

Mounted albumin print from Gardner's Sketch Book, *volume 2, plate 94, entitled* A Burial Party on the Battle-field of Cold Harbor.

WILLIAM W. HEARTSILL'S FAMOUS AND EXCEEDINGLY RARE CONFEDERATE MEMOIR, *FOURTEEN HUNDRED AND 91 DAYS IN THE CONFEDERATE ARMY: A JOURNAL KEPT BY W. W. HEARTSILL FOR FOUR YEARS, ONE MONTH AND ONE DAY. OR, CAMP LIFE, DAY-BY-DAY, OF THE W. P. LANE RANGERS FROM APRIL 19TH, 1861 TO MAY 20TH, 1865* (MARSHALL, TX, 1876).

William Williston Heartsill (1839–1916) printed the one hundred copies of the edition by hand on a small printing press over a period of several years. The result was an unvarnished account of his activities and those of his regiment, the Second Texas Cavalry. Heartsill kept a diary for the entire period, and after the war wrote two separate, and slightly different, manuscripts from them.

Corresponding with fellow members of his unit, the "W. P. Lane Rangers," he secured photographs of sixty-one. Heartsill had these copied, and in each of the hundred copies he printed, he pasted the sixty-one albumin photographs by hand. The book was finished at his home in Marshall, Texas, in July of 1876. It is estimated that fewer than twenty copies survive intact.

ABOVE: *Original binding of Heartsill's* Fourteen Hundred and 91 Days in the Confederate Army. BELOW: *A two-page spread showing portraits of four of Heartsill's comrades.*

FACING PAGE, BELOW: *Hand-mounted photographic frontispiece of Heartsill's* Fourteen Hundred and 91 Days in the Confederate Army.

Title page of Heartsill's Fourteen Hundred and 91 Days in the Confederate Army.

FOURTEEN HUNDRED AND 91 DAYS, IN THE CONFEDERATE ARMY.

A JOURNAL, KEPT BY W. W. HEARTSILL FOR FOUR YEARS, ONE MONTH, AND ONE DAY. OR CAMP LIFE; DAY-BY-DAY, OF THE W. P. LANE RANGERS. FROM APRIL 19th 1861, TO MAY 20th 1865.

W. W. Heartsill.

REMINISCENCES

OF

CONFEDERATE SERVICE,

1861–1865.

BY

CAPT. FRANCIS W. DAWSON, C. S. A.

[100 COPIES.]

CHARLESTON, S. C.
THE NEWS AND COURIER BOOK PRESSES.
1882.

TITLE PAGE OF FRANCIS WARRINGTON DAWSON'S *REMINISCENCES OF CONFEDERATE SERVICE, 1861–1865* (CHARLESTON, SC: THE NEWS AND COURIER BOOK PRESSES, 1882). THE ORIGINAL WAS PRINTED IN AN EDITION OF ONE HUNDRED COPIES FOR PRIVATE CIRCULATION ONLY.

Notable as the only full-length memoir by an Englishman who served the Confederacy, it is among the rarest and most entertaining Confederate narratives. Born Austin John Reeks in London in 1840, Dawson decided to journey to the Confederate states in 1861 to offer his services. One account indicates that he changed his name in the event that his actions might bring shame on the family. An uncle, Captain William A. Dawson, had been killed while serving in India, and his widow had financed young Austin's education.

Through the influence of A. Dudley Mann, a Confederate agent in England, Dawson was able to join the crew of the Confederate steamer *Nashville* as a common sailor. The captain of the *Nashville*, Robert B. Pegram, arranged to have Dawson commissioned a master's mate in the Confederate navy. Doubtful of his ability to obtain a naval officer's commission, Dawson arranged to join an artillery battery commanded by Pegram's nephew.

Through the exertions of his new commander, Captain Willie B. Pegram, and the wife of Judah P. Benjamin, the Confederate secretary of war, Dawson was commissioned a first lieutenant of artillery in 1862.

Serving as an ordnance officer on the staff of General James Longstreet from 1862 to 1864 Dawson requested and received a transfer to the staff of General Fitzhugh Lee, nephew of Robert E. Lee, serving there until the end of the war.

His postwar career as an editor was marked by a push for industrialization of the South, primarily his advocacy for creating a regional textile industry. His support of the overthrow of the radical Reconstruction government of South Carolina brought him into prominence in the state Democratic Party. Dawson was a delegate to the national convention in 1880, 1884, and 1888. In 1874 he married Sarah Fowler Morgan, the sister of his longtime friend James M. Morgan.

Original binding of Francis Warrington Dawson's Reminiscences of Confederate Service, 1861–1865.

First edition of Sarah Morgan Dawson's *A Confederate Girl's Diary* (Boston: Houghton Mifflin Company, 1913). One of the most entertaining memoirs by a Confederate girl, this book is very rarely seen with the original dust jacket.

Sarah Fowler Morgan (1842–1909) was born in New Orleans into a prominent family that suffered tremendous loss during the war. One brother remained loyal to the North; another was killed in a duel in 1861. Her father, Judge Thomas Gibbes Morgan, died in 1862, and of her other three brothers, two were killed fighting for the Confederacy. The remaining brother, James Morris Morgan, a Confederate naval officer, also wrote a Civil War memoir, entitled *Recollections of a Rebel Reefer* (Boston, 1917).

With the occupation of New Orleans Judge Morgan moved the family to Baton Rouge, which was eventually occupied by Union troops in May of 1862. It is at that point that Sarah's diary begins. After an abortive attempt to retake Baton Rouge by the Confederate army in August of 1862, portions of the town, including the Morgan home, were devastated. Refugees for a time Sarah, her mother, and her sisters were forced to return to New Orleans and live with her Unionist brother for the duration of the war. In 1872 the Morgan family moved to Columbia, South Carolina. There Sarah made the acquaintance of Francis Warrington Dawson, the

editor of the *Charleston News & Courier*, and at his request she began writing editorials for that paper under the pen name "Mr. Fowler." Circumstances required another move, this time to Charleston where her friendship with the recently widowed Dawson blossomed into romance, and the couple was married in 1874.

After the murder of her husband in 1889 (the culprit claimed self-defense), Sarah became a veritable recluse for the next ten years. Following her daughter's marriage in 1898, she sold her interest in the *News & Courier* and moved permanently to Paris, France. Her son, Francis Warrington Dawson, arranged for the posthumous publication of her diary.

RIGHT: *Original dust jacket of Dawson's* A Confederate Girl's Diary.

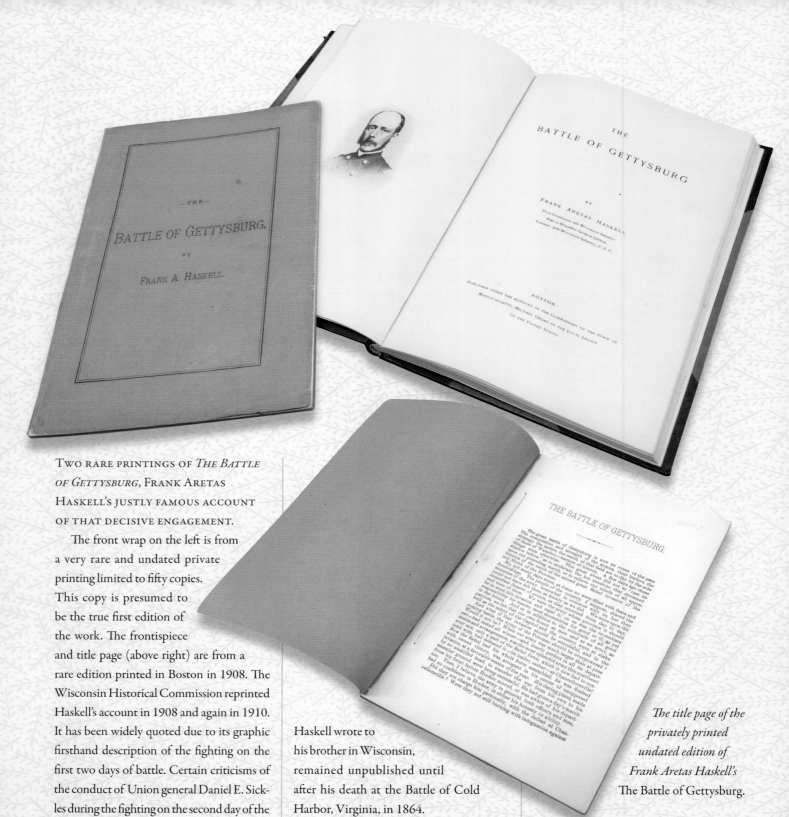

The front wrap on the left is from
a very rare and undated private
printing limited to fifty copies.
This copy is presumed to
be the true first edition of
the work. The frontispiece
and title page (above right) are from a
rare edition printed in Boston in 1908. The
Wisconsin Historical Commission reprinted
Haskell's account in 1908 and again in 1910.
It has been widely quoted due to its graphic
firsthand description of the fighting on the
first two days of battle. Certain criticisms of
the conduct of Union general Daniel E. Sick-
les during the fighting on the second day of the
battle have been deleted from some later printings. Haskell and his account are the subject of
a recent scholarly book *Haskell of Gettysburg:
His Life and Civil War Papers*, edited by Frank
L. Byrne and Andrew T. Weaver.

Frank Aretas Haskell (1828–1864) wrote
what has become perhaps the most quoted
account of the Union repulse of Pickett's
Charge as well as the fighting in Devil's Den
and the Peach Orchard. The account, which

Haskell wrote to
his brother in Wisconsin,
remained unpublished until
after his death at the Battle of Cold
Harbor, Virginia, in 1864.

Haskell was born in Vermont but moved
to Wisconsin to study law in his brother's
Madison practice. With the outbreak of the
war Haskell enlisted in the Sixth Wisconsin
Infantry, which became part of the famed
Iron Brigade. Haskell was serving on the
staff of General John Gibbon, commander
of a division in the Union Second Corps, at
the Battle of Gettysburg. Haskell's account
of the fighting on the second and third days

*The title page of the
privately printed
undated edition of
Frank Aretas Haskell's
The Battle of Gettysburg.*

of the battle (July 2 and 3, 1863) is unvarnished and critical of certain individuals and
commands. Gibbon gave Haskell great credit
for his part in the failure of Pickett's men to
break the Union line. Haskell was eventually promoted to colonel of the Thirty-sixth
Wisconsin Infantry. He was placed in charge
of his unit's brigade upon the death of its
commander at Cold Harbor and within
minutes was himself killed.

TWO RARE PRINTINGS OF *THE BATTLE
OF GETTYSBURG*, FRANK ARETAS
HASKELL'S JUSTLY FAMOUS ACCOUNT
OF THAT DECISIVE ENGAGEMENT.

JOSEPH T. WILSON'S *THE BLACK PHALANX; A HISTORY OF THE NEGRO SOLDIERS OF THE UNITED STATES IN THE WARS OF 1775–1812, 1861–'65* (HARTFORD, CT: AMERICAN PUBLISHING COMPANY, 1888).

Joseph Thomas Wilson (1836–1891), who served in the Second Regiment of the Louisiana Native Guards as well as the famed Fifty-fourth Massachusetts Infantry, is shown in the frontispiece in his Grand Army of the Republic fraternal uniform. He also served as an aide-de-camp to the commander in chief of that organization. Wilson, an already published author, undertook to write this history at the urging of his comrades at the 1882 annual meeting of the Encampment of the Department of Virginia, Grand Army of the Republic at Richmond. His previous works

included *Twenty-Two Years of Freedom, Emancipation*, and *Voice of a New Race*. The two-volume *Civil War Books: A Critical Bibliography*, edited by noted historians Bell I. Wiley, James I. Robertson, and Allan Nevins

called *The Black Phalanx* "a significant work by a former Negro soldier; full of official dispatches and lengthy essays . . . valuable for a discussion of anti-Negro prejudice in the army."

ORIGINAL BINDING OF COLONEL WILLIAM C. OATES'S CIVIL WAR MEMOIR *THE WAR BETWEEN THE UNION AND THE CONFEDERACY AND ITS LOST OPPORTUNITIES* (NEW YORK AND WASHINGTON: THE NEALE PUBLISHING CO., 1905).

William Calvin Oates (1835–1910) was born in Pike County, Alabama, into a poor farming family. Oates was a product of his rough and tumble beginnings, and after committing an assault in 1851 he decided to leave home.

After a three-year stint of living on his own he returned to Alabama, settling in Henry County. Between then and 1858 he eked out a living variously teaching and attending school. In that year he traveled to Eufaula and began to read law in the office of the firm of James Lawrence Pugh, Edward C. Pugh, and Jefferson Buford. After earning his license he established a practice in Abbeville, Henry County, Alabama.

With the outbreak of the war he raised a company of infantry that eventually

became Company G of the Fifteenth Alabama Infantry. Promoted to colonel in January 1863, he led the regiment in the Battle of Gettysburg. Oates and the Fifteenth Alabama were involved in the desperate fighting around Little Round Top against Colonel Joshua Chamberlain and the Twentieth Maine. Wounded at the Battle of Chickamauga in September, 1863, he returned to his regiment in the spring of 1864 but was supplanted in command in August, being given command of another Alabama regiment. A wound that month necessitated the amputation of his right arm.

After the war he reestablished his law practice and was elected to the US House of Representatives in 1880. Oates ran for governor in 1894 and defeated Reuben F. Kolb of Eufaula, possibly due to ballot

fraud. Oates held no further public offices after 1896 and devoted his declining years to Confederate reunions and the writing of his Civil War memoirs.

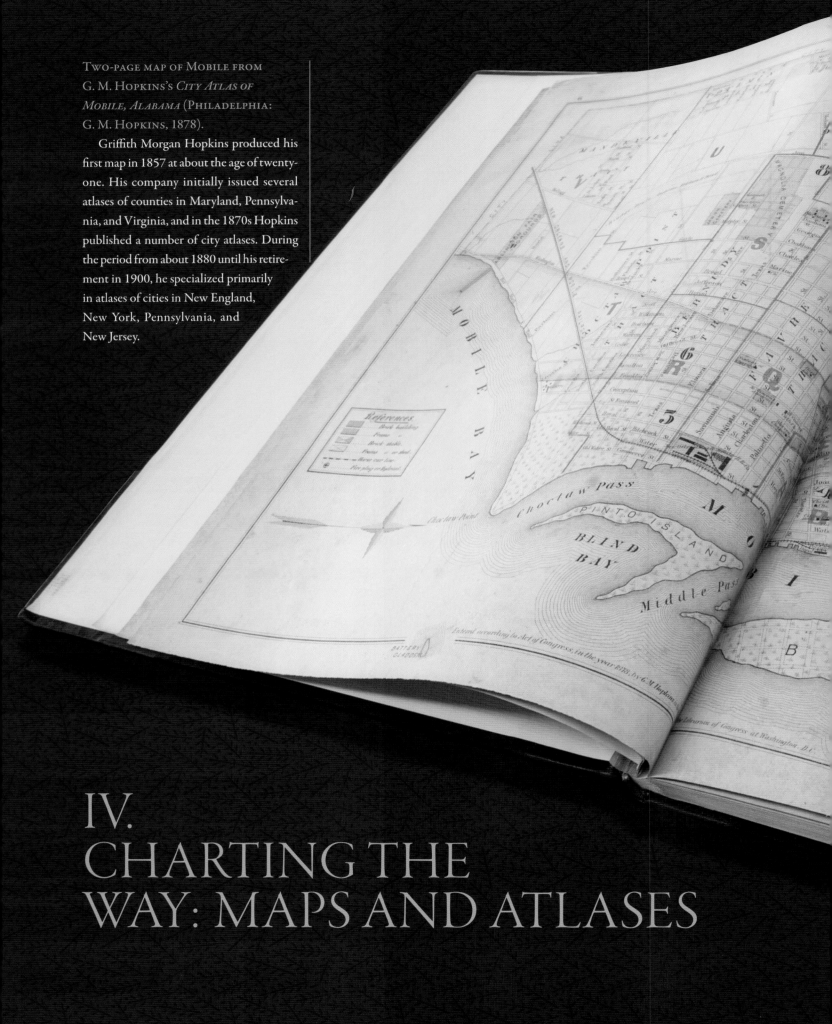

Griffith Morgan Hopkins produced his
first map in 1857 at about the age of twenty-
one. His company initially issued several
atlases of counties in Maryland, Pennsylvania, and Virginia, and in the 1870s Hopkins
published a number of city atlases. During
the period from about 1880 until his retirement in 1900, he specialized primarily
in atlases of cities in New England,
New York, Pennsylvania, and
New Jersey.

IV.
CHARTING THE
WAY: MAPS AND ATLASES

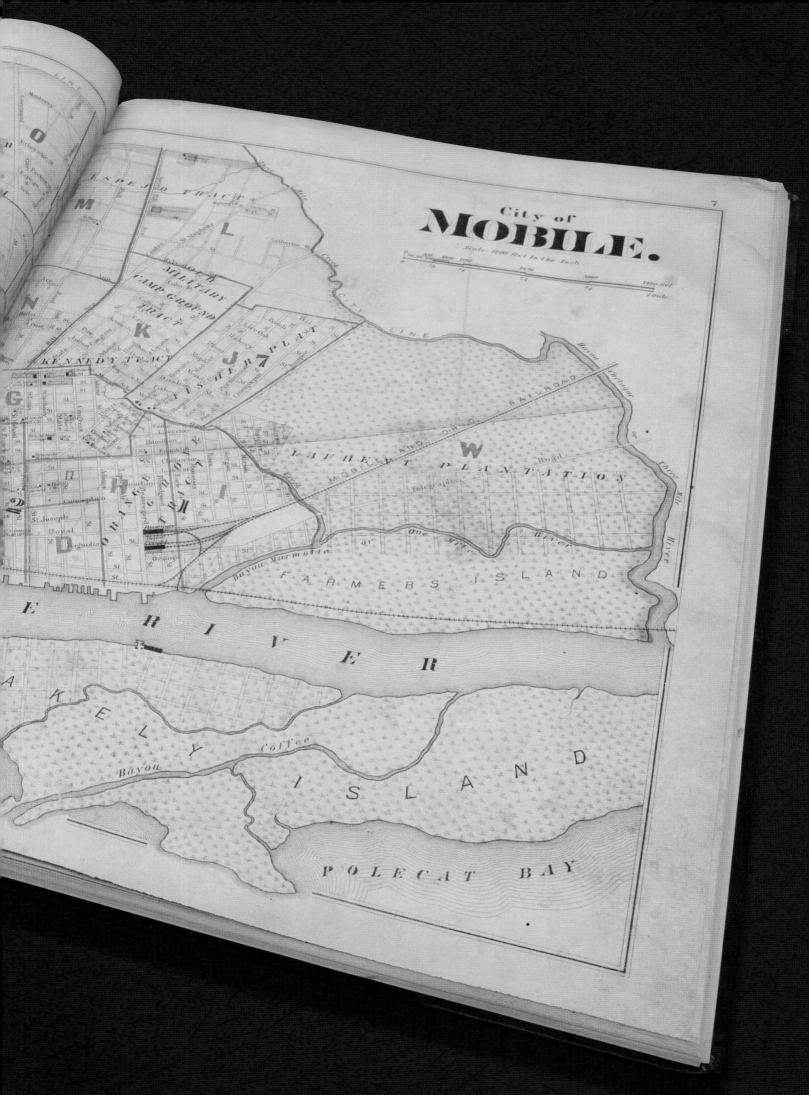

City of
MOBILE.

Scale 1200 feet to the Inch

I̲N ADDITION TO AN IMPORTANT collection of Civil War maps, the A. S. Williams III Americana Collection contains an excellent group of maps relating to virtually all periods of Alabama history and smaller but significant groups relating to the United States and the Southeast. There are a number of early world and US atlases as well as a number of atlases, insurance maps, and promotional publications relating to Alabama towns and cities from the 1870s to the 1920s. The map collection also holds a set of the rare *Atlas to Accompany the Official Records of the War of the Rebellion* and a number of important maps printed in the Confederacy.

PLATE TWENTY-FOUR OF *A NEW GENERAL ATLAS, COMPRISING A COMPLETE SET OF MAPS, REPRESENTING THE GRAND DIVISIONS OF THE GLOBE, TOGETHER WITH THE SEVERAL EMPIRES, KINGDOMS AND STATES IN THE WORLD: COMPILED FROM THE BEST AUTHORITIES, AND CORRECTED BY THE MOST RECENT DISCOVERIES* (1824).

This very fine example of a map of Alabama by noted cartographer Anthony Finley, issued in Philadelphia in 1824, measures ten and three-quarter inches by eight and one-quarter inches and is hand colored.

Anthony Finley (c.1790–1840) published several editions of his *New General Atlas* between 1818 and 1834.

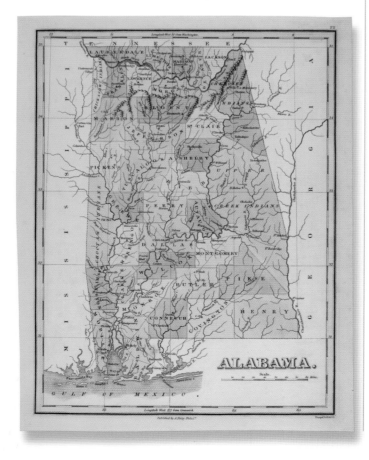

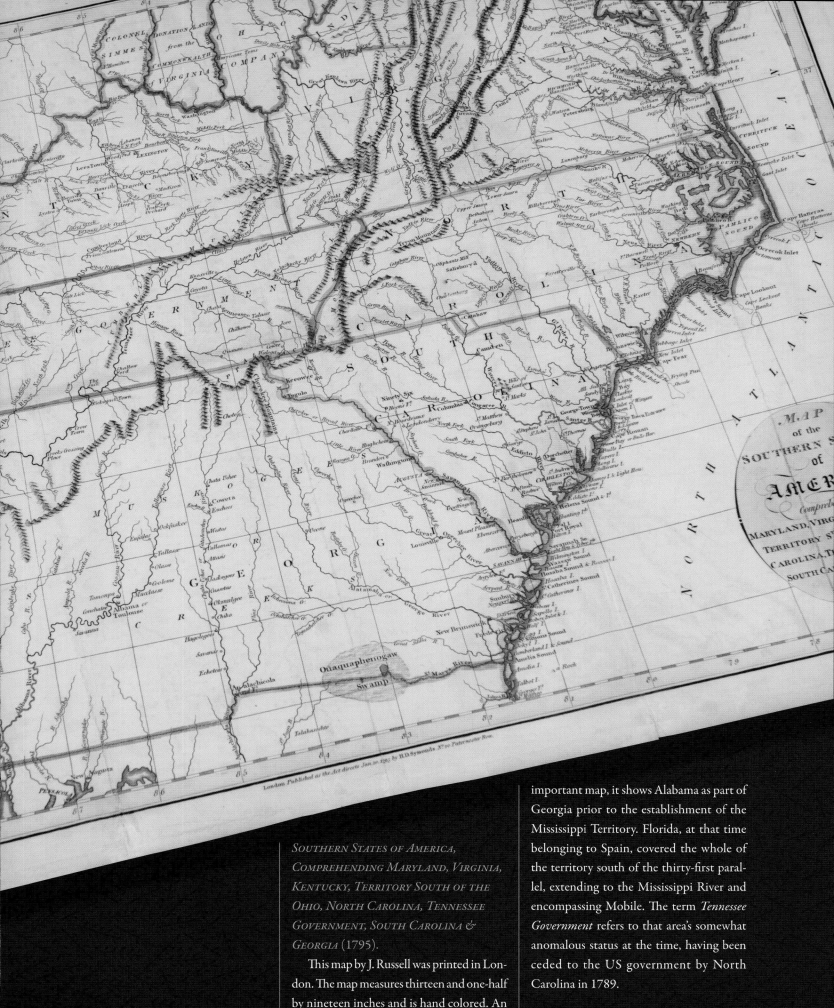

Southern States of America, Comprehending Maryland, Virginia, Kentucky, Territory South of the Ohio, North Carolina, Tennessee Government, South Carolina & Georgia (1795).

This map by J. Russell was printed in London. The map measures thirteen and one-half by nineteen inches and is hand colored. An important map, it shows Alabama as part of Georgia prior to the establishment of the Mississippi Territory. Florida, at that time belonging to Spain, covered the whole of the territory south of the thirty-first parallel, extending to the Mississippi River and encompassing Mobile. The term *Tennessee Government* refers to that area's somewhat anomalous status at the time, having been ceded to the US government by North Carolina in 1789.

A New Map of Part of the United States of North America. Containing the Carolinas and Georgia. Also the Floridas and Part of the Bahama Islands &c (1825).

Issued by John Cary in 1825, this map is noted as being "from the Latest Authorities." The map is seventeen inches by nineteen and one-half inches and is hand colored.

By 1825, six years after statehood, Alabama was considerably larger than its current boundaries. However, West Florida had declared itself an independent republic in 1810 but was soon after annexed by the United States. With the Adams-Onis Treaty of 1819 Spain ceded both East and West Florida to the United States. The treaty took effect in 1821, and the federal government established the basic state boundaries we have today. The Florida Territory was organized in 1822, and statehood followed in 1845.

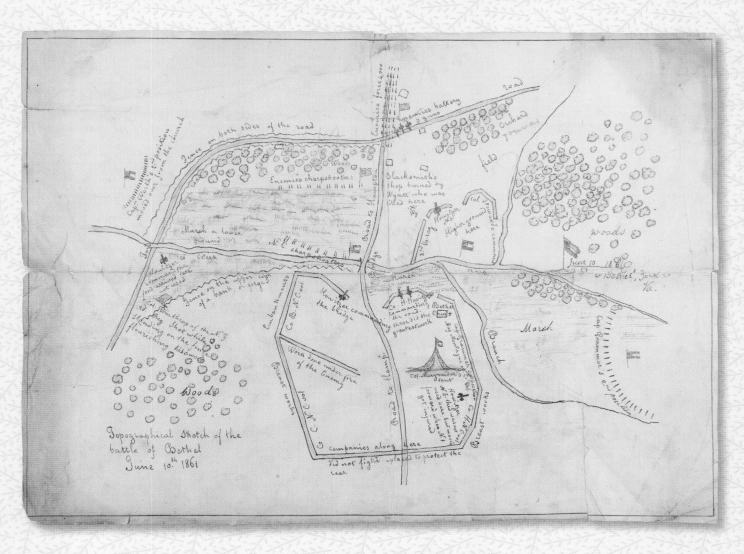

Topographical Sketch of the battle of Bethel June 10th 1861

TOPOGRAPHICAL SKETCH OF THE BATTLE OF BETHEL JUNE 10TH, 1861 (1861?).

The Williams copy of this Confederate imprint has apparently had its original margins trimmed and has been hand colored.

The battle of Big Bethel, Virginia, was the result of a reconnaisance in force by Union troops stationed at Fort Monroe, Virginia. Little more than a skirmish, it resulted in the Union forces withdrawing back to their base with total casualties of 18 killed, 53 wounded, and 5 missing out of a force of 2,500. The Confederate force of 1,200 suffered losses of 1 killed and 7 wounded. What the battle lacked in bloodshed was more than sufficiently made up for in a boost to Confederate morale and a consequential dampening of Union spirits.

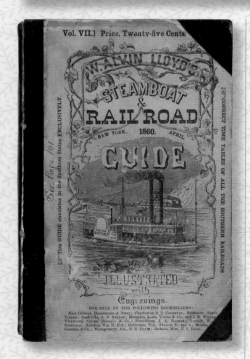

Front cover of the April 1860 volume of W. Alvin Lloyd's Steamboat and Rail Road Guide.

W. ALVIN LLOYD'S SOUTHERN RAIL ROAD MAP (1863).

This rare Confederate imprint map was copyrighted in Mobile in 1863 by W. Alvin Lloyd and lithographed in Mobile by W. R. Robertson under an 1865 date. There are only three other known copies in institutions, and this copy is the only one in Alabama. The map is hand colored and measures 43.5 by 58.5 centimeters.

William Alvin Lloyd (?–1868) was a publisher of railroad and steamboat timetables for the Southern states before the Civil War. An account by modern author Donald E. Markle has Lloyd receiving a passport from Abraham Lincoln to travel in the South to further his publishing activities. With this passport came the proviso that he was to be a personal spy for Lincoln and was to communicate only with him. Purportedly Lloyd and two associates traveled the Confederacy for four years and provided Lincoln with certain military intelligence, improbable though this seems.

TITLE PAGE OF G. M. HOPKINS'S *CITY ATLAS OF MOBILE, ALABAMA* (PHILADELPHIA: G. M. HOPKINS, 1878).

This highly detailed atlas with delineations between brick and frame buildings includes residences and other type buildings, the location of fire plugs or hydrants, the location of the horse car line, and identifies some owners of buildings or property.

BELOW: *Map of part of wards 3, 4, and 6 from Hopkins's* City Atlas of Mobile, Alabama. *The Catholic cathedral is in the upper left-hand corner.*

RIGHT: *Original binding of Hopkins's* City Atlas of Mobile, Alabama.

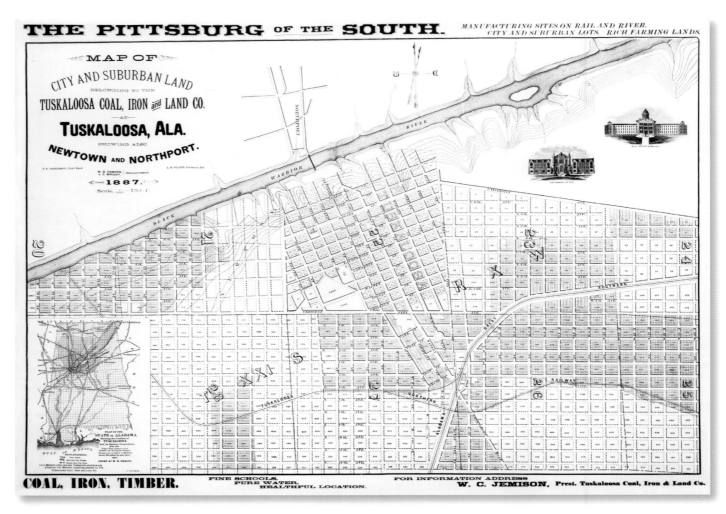

THE PITTSBURG OF THE SOUTH.
MANUFACTURING SITES ON RAIL AND RIVER.
CITY AND SUBURBAN LOTS. RICH FARMING LANDS.

MAP OF CITY AND SUBURBAN LAND BELONGING TO THE TUSKALOOSA COAL, IRON and LAND CO. AT TUSKALOOSA, ALA. SHOWING ALSO NEWTOWN AND NORTHPORT. 1887.

COAL, IRON, TIMBER.
FINE SCHOOLS. PURE WATER. HEALTHFUL LOCATION.
FOR INFORMATION ADDRESS W. C. JEMISON, Prest. Tuskaloosa Coal, Iron & Land Co.

The Pittsburg of the South. City and Suburban Land Belonging to the Tuskaloosa Coal Iron and Land Co. Tuskaloosa, Ala. Showing Also Newtown and Northport (1887).

This map measures twenty by twenty-eight inches. Issued to promote the relocation of businesses and individuals to the city, it shows both the University of Alabama and the Alabama Insane Hospital in vignettes in the upper right corner. The president of the Tuskaloosa Coal Iron and Land Company was Tuscaloosa native W. C. Jemison.

William Carlos Jemison (1850–1901) was most notably a newspaper editor and twice mayor of Tuscaloosa. Jemison graduated from the University of Alabama with a law degree in 1874 but left that field to engage in the coal and iron business. He was mayor of Tuscaloosa from 1889 to 1890 and again from 1894 to 1900. Jemison's notable accomplishments included establishing a system of graded public schools and barge line communication with Mobile. At the time of his death he was editor and proprietor of the *Tuscaloosa Times.*

Tuscaloosa District of Alabama (Mobile: Press of Gill Printing Co., 1915).

A brochure published by the Tuscaloosa Board of Trade, illustrated and compiled by G. Guild.

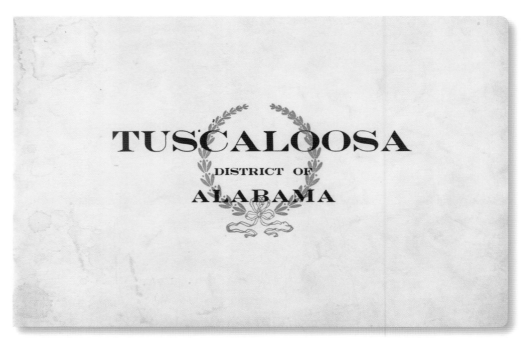

TUSCALOOSA DISTRICT OF ALABAMA

Brochure for the Hotel Monte Sano, near Huntsville, Alabama.

Huntsville is characterized on the reverse as (of course) the "Loveliest City of the South." This publication was issued by the North Alabama Improvement Company in 1888 and was illustrated and printed by the South Publishing Co., 76 Park Place, New York.

Right: *Back cover of the Hotel Monte Sano brochure.*

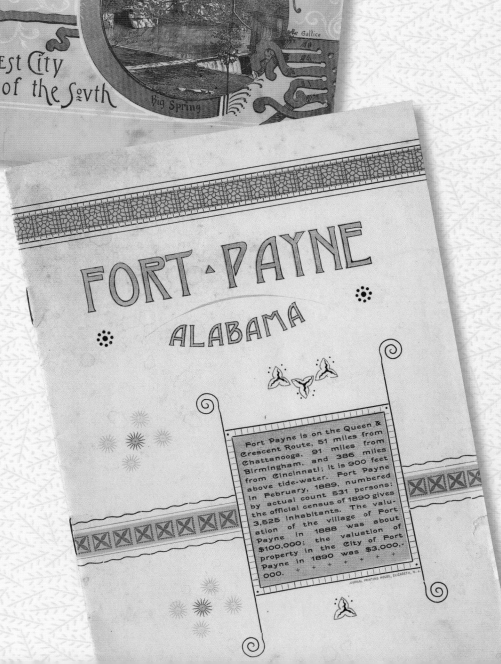

An attractive promotional brochure for Fort Payne, Alabama, published by the Fort Payne Coal and Iron Company in 1890.

The center box has a number of interesting facts, including the distance between Fort Payne and Cincinnati, that Fort Payne's elevation is nine hundred feet above tidewater, and that the rush has begun. The population of Fort Payne by actual count in 1889 was 531 inhabitants, but the official census of 1890 puts that figure at 3,525. Fort Payne ho!

SHEFFIELD, ALABAMA. THE IRON MANUFACTURING CENTER OF THE SOUTH ON THE TENNESSEE RIVER. ITS WONDERFUL RESOURCES, ADVANTAGES AND PROSPECTS.

This publication was issued by the Sheffield Land, Iron and Coal Company in 1889 and was printed by the South Publishing Co., 76 Park Place, New York.

LADY ENSLEY FURNACE. DAILY CAPACITY 125 TONS.

ABOVE: *Interior illustration from* Sheffield, Alabama.

Interior spread (above) and cover (below) from Sheffield, Alabama.

BELOW: A WELL-ILLUSTRATED BROCHURE TOUTING BIRMINGHAM. *VIEWS OF BIRMINGHAM, ALABAMA, WITH A GLIMPSE AT SOME OF THE NATURAL RESOURCES OF THE BIRMINGHAM DISTRICT AND THE INDUSTRIES BASED THEREON* (NEW YORK AND NEW ORLEANS: ISIDORE NEWMAN & SON, BANKERS,1908).

Isidore Newman (1837–1909) established a private, nondenominational, coeducational college preparatory school in New Orleans in 1903. Newman, a New Orleans businessman and founder of the Maison Blanche department store chain, originally founded the school to provide for academic and practical training for children at the Jewish Orphans Home. The school changed its name—to the Isidore Newman School—and direction in 1931. Distinguished alumni include Harry Connick Jr. as well as Peyton and Eli Manning.

ABOVE: FRONT AND BACK COVER FOR *CITRONELLE: IN THE PINES OF ALABAMA.*

The Passenger Department of the Mobile and Ohio Railroad could not say enough about Citronelle, Alabama, in this 1903 publication. Noting its reputation as a health resort, the brochure went on to say that it had the purest water in the United States! An analysis by a respected laboratory concluded that the water there was "99.99968% pure."

V.
PEOPLE AND PLACES: PRINTS, POSTCARDS, AND RELATED GRAPHICS

PADDY CARR.

CREEK INTERPRETER.

PUBLISHED BY F. W. GREENOUGH, PHILAD.

Printed & Coloured at J.T.Bowen's Lithographic Establishment No 94 Walnut St.

Congress in the Year 1838 by F Worromough in the Clerks Office of the District Court of the Eastern District of Penn.

T HE A. S. WILLIAMS III Americana Collection includes numerous prints, which focus primarily on important figures of American history, from presidents and generals to statesman and other prominent personalities. The Civil War is well represented with prints featuring individuals, battle scenes, naval themes, and several fine panoramic views. The collection houses two important Civil War–related portfolios—A. J. Volck's *Confederate War Etchings* and J. Nep Roesler's *War Scenes, Sketched from Nature and Drawn on Stone*—as well as a group of original proof copies of illustrations by John W. Evans for the Cen-

tury Company's monumental publication *Battles and Leaders of the Civil War*. Two important prints depicting George Washington are also included. One, by Valentine Green and based on a John Trumbull painting, was published in London in 1781; the other, by French artist Noel Le Mire, appeared in Paris in 1780. Other groupings include political broadsides, cartoons, and modern Civil War prints. Postcards form an important addition to the graphics collection. Based heavily on Southern themes and the Civil War, the postcard collection also contains an outstanding archive of Alabama-related real photo cards.

GENERAL WASHINGTON.

LEFT: *GENERAL WASHINGTON*, MEZZOTINT ENGRAVING BY VALENTINE GREEN, PUBLISHED IN LONDON IN 1781.

This rare and beautiful mezzotint engraving is the work of Valentine Green (1739–1813), a fashionable London printmaker who styled himself "Mezzotinto Engraver to His Majesty & to the Elector Palatine." The engraving is based on a painting by John Trumbull (1756–1843), called "the painter of the Revolution" and an aide-de-camp to Washington during the war. Trumbull painted Washington from memory in London in 1780, and the work was subsequently sold to an Amsterdam banker, one M. De Neufville. Before it left England, it was engraved by Green, who published it under the date of January 15, 1781.

FACING PAGE: *SPRING FROG: A CHEROKEE CHIEF*, 1838.

Print from F. W. Greenough's rare printing of Thomas L. McKenney and James L. Hall's *History of the Indian Tribes of North America, with Biographical Sketches and Anecdotes of the Principal Chiefs* (Philadelphia: F. W. Greenough, 1838–1844).

Tooan Tuh or Spring Frog (1754–1859) was born near Lookout Mountain, within the boundaries of the state of Tennessee, and was a chief of the Cherokees. He apparently possessed a remarkable physique and excelled at a Native American ball game that most resembles modern lacrosse. In 1818, though sixty-four at the time, Tooan Tuh accompanied a band of Creek warriors on a war party against a band of Osage Indians. He served under Andrew Jackson during the Creek Wars, being present at the battles of Emuckfaw and Horseshoe Bend. Tooan Tuh was one of the earliest of the Cherokees to immigrate to the tribal lands set aside in Arkansas. His death by drowning occurred near Briartown, Oklahoma.

SPRING FROG

A CHEROKEE CHIEF.

PUBLISHED BY F. W. GREENOUGH, PHILAD.a

Drawn Printed & Coloured at I.T.Bowen's Lithographic Establishment N.º 94 Walnut St.

Entered according to act of Congress in the Year 1838 by F. Greenough, in the Clerks Office of the District Court of the Eastern District of Penn.a

TOMPKIN'S FARM.
(Camp Gauley View)

LITHOGRAPHIC ILLUSTRATION
TOMPKINS FARM (CAMP GAULEY MOUNTAIN) PUBLISHED IN J. NEP. ROESLER'S *WAR SCENES, SKETCHED FROM NATURE AND DRAWN ON STONE* (CINCINNATI: PRINTED BY EHRGOTT, FORBRIGER, 1862).

As an infantryman in the Forty-seventh Ohio Infantry, J. Nep Roesler participated in the 1861 campaign in western Virginia. Little is known of his background or subsequent career. Mark Neely and Harold Holzer devote eight pages to Roesler in their book *The Union Image: Popular Prints of the Civil War North*. Five of the twenty images from Roesler's 1862 work are included, and Neely and Holzer believe the quality of the images and their early appearance should have resulted in a commercial success. However, few copies of the original exist today.

JOHN W. EVANS'S *BATTLE OF MOBILE BAY* AFTER A PAINTING BY J. O. DAVIDSON.

John William Evans (1855–1943) was an American engraver. The Williams Collection has a group of eighteen original proof copies of illustrations Evans created for *Battles and Leaders of the Civil War* (New York: Century Company, 1884–1887). Each engraving is signed in pencil by Evans, and subjects include naval scenes, battlefield scenes, and portraits of general officers, including William Tecumseh Sherman and Philip Henry Sheridan.

Offering of Bells to Be Cast into Cannon.

One of the more often reproduced etchings from Adalbert John Volck's *Confederate War Etchings* (Philadelphia, c. 1880).

Adalbert Johann Volck (1828–1912) was a native of Bavaria and educated in Germany. His sympathies with the spirit of revolt in that country in 1848 forced his immigration to the United States the following year. After a brief participation in the gold rush, Volck moved to Maryland and entered the Baltimore College of Dental Surgery. Upon graduation he became a lifelong resident of that city and was a charter member of the Maryland State Dental Association.

Volck was an ardent Southern sympathizer and was instrumental in the effort by like-minded Marylanders to smuggle medicine into the South. The anti-Southern caricatures of Thomas Nast spurred Volck to prepare his *Confederate War Etchings* using the pseudonym "V. Blada." Publishing these caricatures under his own name would likely have led to his arrest and possible imprisonment. The twenty-nine illustrations present both a violent prejudice against the North as well as depictions of Southern sacrifice and unity. The set in the Williams Collection is a reissue from the 1880s of the originals issued during the war.

MONTGOMERY GREYS, CO. A 2ND REGT. A.S.T. * CAPT. AMERINE.

ALA. STATE ARTILLERY CO. G. 1ST REGT. A.S.T. · CAPT. C. L. HUGER

TWO COLORED LITHOGRAPHS THAT ORIGINALLY APPEARED IN THOMAS COOPER DELEON'S *THE SOLDIER'S SOUVENIR OF THE INTERSTATE DRILL AND ENCAMPMENT: CAMP R. C. DRUM, MOBILE, ALA., WEEK OF MAY 4TH, 1885* (MOBILE: JOHN L. RAPIER, 1885).

The complete volume is exceptionally rare. State and city militia units and drill teams came to Mobile to participate in a display of organizational efficiency and discipline. These units, most attached to the National Guard of their respective states, were drawn primarily from the South, with notable exceptions from Wisconsin and Illinois. The ostensible object of the drill was to convince the US War Department of the military value of these units. A similar national drill was held in Washington in 1887.

Thomas Cooper DeLeon (1839–1914) was a prominent author and editor. Born in Columbia, South Carolina, he served in the Confederate army and in 1868 took up residence in Mobile. He worked with John Forsyth on the *Mobile Register* and edited several other publications. In 1873 he brought about a new organization for the Mobile Mardi Gras and managed it for twenty-five years. Among his numerous publications two of the better known involve the Confederacy, *Four Years in Rebel Capitals: An Inside View of Life in the Southern Confederacy, from Birth to Death* (1890) and *Belles, Beaux and Brains of the 60s* (1909).

Eugene A. Smith

PHOTOGRAPHIC PORTRAIT OF
EUGENE A. SMITH WITH A FACSIMILE
SIGNATURE.

Eugene Allen Smith (1841–1927), a native of Autauga County, was educated in the private schools there. After attending public school in Philadelphia, Pennsylvania, he entered the University of Alabama in 1860 receiving the AB degree in 1862. That year he was sent out with the other cadets of his class to drill recruits for the Confederate army. Smith was later detailed as state captain and instructor in tactics at the university and served in that capacity until 1865.

His postwar career as a college professor, naturalist, and geologist was most distinguished. With the reopening of the University of Alabama in 1871, he accepted the position of professor of agricultural chemistry and mineralogy. Smith was appointed state geologist in 1873. Part of his mandate was to travel the state identifying natural resources that could be profitably exploited. His findings and reports influenced northern industrialists and were instrumental in establishing the coal and iron industry as well as other industries in the state. Perhaps his crowning achievement was securing an annual appropriation for the Geological Survey of Alabama, giving financial security to that important organization.

$200 REWARD

For the arrest and conviction, or information that will lead to the arrest and conviction of J. M. Lammons, absconding Superintendent of Education of Geneva, Ala. Left Montgomery on February 20th. Supposed to be in some Southern town.

Twenty-six years old, 5 feet 6 inches high, weighs 120 lbs. Dark complexion, brown eyes, black hair, smooth face. Has spot of gray hair on left side of head.

Took with him his one year old baby and wife who is about the same height as he but heavier, and said to be a fine looking woman.

LOUIS V. CLARK & CO.
STATE AGENTS
THE UNITED STATES FIDELITY & GUARANTY CO.
BIRMINGHAM, ALA.

March 24, 1909.

ABOVE: REWARD POSTER FROM 1909 REGARDING ONE J. M. LAMMONS, SUPERINTENDENT OF EDUCATION OF GENEVA, ALABAMA.

Lammons apparently absconded from the area with something of value. The poster goes on to say that he "took with him his one year old baby and wife who is about the same height as he but heavier, and is said to be a fine looking woman."

BELOW: 1904 REWARD POSTER FROM ATHENS, ALABAMA.

The poster seeks the arrest of one Ed Jarratt for the brutal murder of Mark Yarborough, a young African American.

$125.00
REWARD!

Athens, Ala., June 22, 1904.

A reward of One Hundred and Twenty-five Dollars will be paid for the arrest and delivery to the Sheriff of Limestone county, Alabama, of

one Ed. JARRATT,

who brutally murdered a negro boy named Mark Yarbrough, on the afternoon of June 11, 1904, in this county. One Hundred of this reward is offered by the Governor of the State of Alabama, and Twenty-five by me, as Sheriff of Limestone county.

DESCRIPTION—Ed. Jarratt is about 18 or 20 years old, will weigh about 150 pounds, about 5 feet, 8 or 10 inches tall; not sure whether eyes are blue or brown, has a rough, bumpy face, a little red; sallow complexion; dark hair; has a scar across his left wrist, think the leaders have been cut. Wire any information to

E. F. PURYEAR,

Sheriff Limestone county, ATHENS, ALA.

"Dexter Avenue, looking east showing Fountain and Capitol, Montgomery, Ala."

GROUP OF ALABAMA-RELATED POSTCARDS DATING FROM 1900 TO 1914.

Clockwise from top left: "Dexter Avenue, looking east showing Fountain and Capitol, Montgomery, Ala."; "First House built in Birmingham, Ala., 1869"; "Confederate Monument and Bluff City Inn, Eufaula, Ala."; "Washington Street, Looking North, Marion, Ala."; "Cotton Gin, Marion, Ala."; "Colbert Co. Court House, Tuscumbia, Ala."

Colbert Co. Court House, Tuscumbia, Ala.

First House built in Birmingham, Ala., 1869.

Cotton Gin, Marion, Ala.

CONFEDERATE MONUMENT AND BLUFF CITY INN, EUFAULA, ALA.

Washington Street, Looking North, Marion, Ala.

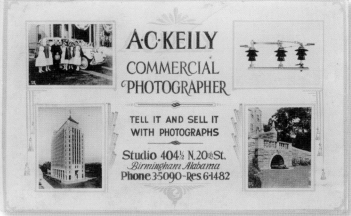

REAL PHOTO POSTCARD
OF THE CAMPUS OF THE MT. VERNON
HOSPITAL, FOUNDED IN 1900.

Mr. Vernon Hospital was the second hospital in the state for the treatment of the mentally ill and was founded on the campus of the old Mt. Vernon Arsenal, which was established in 1828. It was renamed Searcy Hospital in 1919, in honor of Dr. James Thomas Searcy, the second superintendent of the first state mental hospital now Bryce Hospital, which was founded in 1852. Searcy Hospital eventually housed only African American patients until it was desegregated in 1965.

The original barracks of the Mt. Vernon Arsenal still stand, and from 1887 to 1894 they were used to house captured Apache Indians. Geronimo was transferred there from Fort Pickens, near Pensacola, Florida, and reunited with his family, which had been incarcerated at Fort Marion, St. Augustine, Florida. Geronimo remained at Mt. Vernon with his family from 1887 to 1894, at which time he was transferred to Fort Sill, Oklahoma.

PROMOTIONAL POSTCARD FOR
A. C. KEILY'S PHOTOGRAPHIC STUDIO.

Alfred C. "Argo" Keily Jr. (1908–2004) maintained a studio in Birmingham from about 1927 to the mid-1970s. It is assumed he learned the trade from his father, Alfred C. Keily Sr. (?–1926) who moved to Birmingham from Georgia in the 1920s. Keily Jr. was president of the Professional Photographers of Alabama and Mississippi in 1953. The Birmingham Public Library holds a collection of his prints.

MAN VERSUS FISH, REAL PHOTO
POSTCARD.

Mr. W. G. Oliver of Birmingham caught this 215-pound tarpon on August 31, 1916, near the Rolston Hotel at Coden, Alabama. The fish measured six feet eleven inches with a girth of forty-three inches.

REAL PHOTO POSTCARD VIEW OF
WATER STREET LOOKING EAST ON
DAUPHIN STREET, MOBILE.

Presumably taken after post-hurricane flooding, this card was one of a series published and sold by the E. O. Zadek Jewelry Company of Mobile.

Emil Oscar Zadek (c.1841–1908) was a native of Gleiwitz, Prussia, who arrived in America about 1859. He was reportedly an officer in the Mobile Home Guards during the Civil War. Zadek married Elizabeth Bromberg of Mobile in 1866 and entered the jewelry business at that time. Zadek was a Catholic and sang in the cathedral choir. He was also president of the Mobile Frohsinn, a German-American singing society.

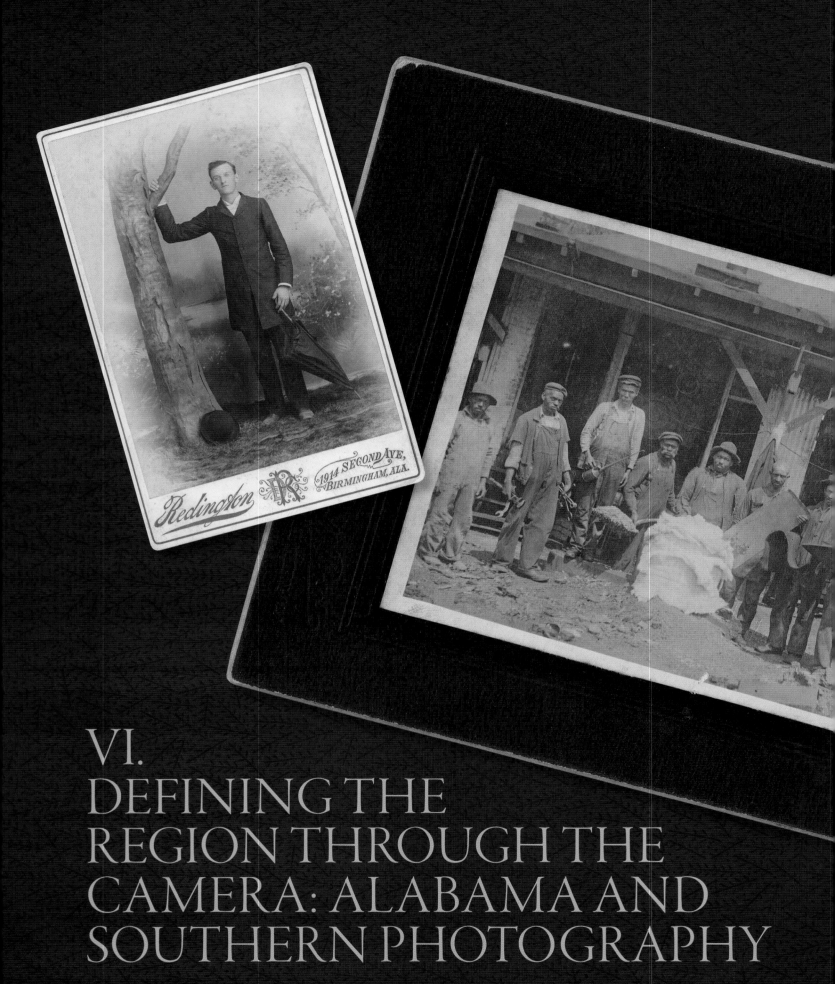

VI.
DEFINING THE
REGION THROUGH THE
CAMERA: ALABAMA AND
SOUTHERN PHOTOGRAPHY

SOUTHERN PHOTOGRAPHS FROM
THE WILLIAMS COLLECTION.

The Williams Collection contains thousands of photographs, including this cabinet card of a dapper young gentleman photographed by D. C. Redington, whose studio was on 1914 Second Avenue, Birmingham, Alabama (facing page, left); two large format photographs from the Russell Bros. Studio in Anniston, Alabama: an industrial scene with African American workers (facing page, right) and the Anniston police department, circa 1900–1910 (top); and a pair of carte de visites (left).

The A. S. Williams III
Americana Collection is home to a most important archive of southern photography. In addition to the extensive collection of Civil War photographs, the archive covers three major categories: the work of southern photographers from 1860 to 1910; life in Alabama over the same general period; and general southern photography. The Southern Photographer, 1860–1910, a collection focusing on southern photographers and their studios is one of the most comprehensive in institutional hands. Covering primarily the period of the carte de visite, cabinet card, and stereoview, the collection documents workplace and work period. It represents photographers and their studios from Maryland, Virginia, North Carolina, South Carolina, Tennessee, Georgia, Alabama, Mississippi, Louisiana, Arkansas, Texas, Kentucky, Missouri, and West Virginia. This part of the collection is comprised of approximately 4,000 images, documenting about 2,500 different studios. Adding to the research value of this archive is a collection of reference materials including books, articles, and biographical sketches of southern photographers. The archive is augmented by a small collection of daguerreotypes and ambrotypes. The photographs of Alabama and the general South are both extensive and varied, and include images into the mid-twentieth century.

Facing page: Daguerreotype taken by African American photographer Augustus Washington.

Augustus Washington (1820/21–1875), the son of a former slave, was born in Trenton, New Jersey. Admitted to Dartmouth College in 1843, he learned the art of daguerrian photography during his freshman year. Leaving college in 1844 Washington moved to Hartford, Connecticut, and began teaching in a school for black students. In 1846 he opened a daguerrean studio in Hartford, one of the city's first.

Washington was quite successful and attracted a broad clientele, as evidenced by this image of a white woman. However, he was unhappy with the social barriers and decided to move to the West African nation of Liberia. Arriving with his family in 1853 he established a daguerrean studio there and eventually operated branch studios in Sierra Leone, Gambia, and Senegal. Washington eventually turned his attention to farming and became one of Liberia's principal sugarcane growers. He served in the Liberian senate and house of representatives before his death in Monrovia.

Above: *Hand-tinted tintype of a young girl from Charles Campbell's gallery in Petersburg, Virginia.*

EXAMPLES OF CARTES DE VISITE FROM VARIOUS ALABAMA PHOTOGRAPHIC STUDIOS. THE CARTE DE VISITE BECAME POPULAR IN THE UNITED STATES ABOUT 1860.

These, along with the cabinet cards and tintypes, comprise part of the Williams Collection archive entitled the Southern Photographer, 1860–1910. This portion of the collection numbers about 4,000 images and documents the activities of about 2,500 different studios from fourteen states. Of interest in this group are two photographs of John Wesley Durr Jr. The first (upper right) shows him on his rocking horse as a child. The second (center right) was taken while Durr was a student at the University of Alabama. Durr (1863–1941) came from a prominent Montgomery family and attended the University of Alabama in 1882. He was variously engaged in the wholesale grocery and wholesale drug business in Montgomery where he founded his own firm, Durr Drug Company.

The carte de visite (below) from Collins' Excelsior Gallery in Huntsville, Alabama, is approximately life-size.

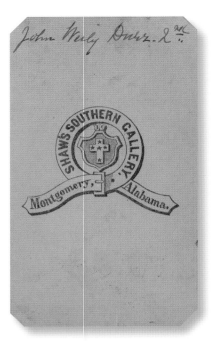

INTRODUCED ABOUT A DECADE AFTER
THE CARTE DE VISITE, THE CABINET
CARD FEATURED A MUCH LARGER
IMAGE.

Clockwise from top: Two cadets photographed by H. P. Tresslar in 1888 at his studio at 10 Court Square in Montgomery; a pair of attractive young ladies photographed at the Tuscaloosa studio of F. M. Turner; an example of customer loyalty: these two photographs were both taken by the T. J. Fitzpatrick studio in Bessemer, Alabama, several years apart.

CARTE DE VISITE OF THE
INTERIOR OF THE
DOWNTOWN FIRST BAPTIST
CHURCH ON CANAL STREET,
MOBILE.

The photographer was Chaun-
cey Barnes, whose studio was at 87
Dauphin Street.

CARTE DE VISITE OF THE
CITY EXCHANGE IN SAVANNAH,
GEORGIA, TAKEN CIRCA 1870.

The photographer was with Perry and
Loveridge's Forest City Gallery at 140
Broughton Street.

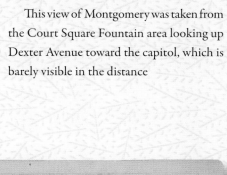

STEREOVIEW OF MONTGOMERY.
This view of Montgomery was taken from the Court Square Fountain area looking up Dexter Avenue toward the capitol, which is barely visible in the distance

DEXTER AVENUE IN MONTGOMERY LOOKING TOWARD THE STATE CAPITOL, 1890s.

ABOVE: PHOTOGRAPH OF THE BIRMINGHAM RIFLES VERNON TEAM, AUGUST 1, 1889, TAKEN BY D. C. REDINGTON, SECOND AVENUE, BIRMINGHAM, ALABAMA.

This detachment of the Birmingham Rifles was sent to Vernon in Lamar County, Alabama, to prevent an outbreak of vigilantism. The notorious outlaw Rube Burrow was suspected of murdering Moses Graves, the postmaster in Jewel, Alabama. Burrow was not arrested, but his father, Allen Burrow, and brother John were apprehended, along with James Cash, a brother-in-law, and charged as accomplices. Fearful of a possible lynching, the local sheriff called on the governor for assistance, and the Birmingham Rifles were dispatched. The captain of the Vernon Team, S. D. Weakley, incidentally, was the city attorney of Birmingham. No proof being offered by the local prosecutor, the three were released.

BELOW: THE DEMOPOLIS, ALABAMA, HOME GUARD PRIOR TO THE SPANISH-AMERICAN WAR.

ALABAMA POLYTECHNIC INSTITUTE (NOW AUBURN UNIVERSITY) FACULTY, CIRCA 1899.

Second from the left in the front row is Dr. William LeRoy Broun (1827–1902), a native of Virginia, former Confederate ordnance officer and president of the school, and third from left is Otis Davis Smith (1831–1905) formerly professor of English but professor of mathematics when this picture was taken. The gentleman to the far right is James Henry Lane (1833–1907), also a native of Virginia and a graduate of the Virginia Military Institute. Lane was a brigadier-general in the Confederate army and was professor of civil engineering.

First on the left in the second row is Charles Hunter Ross (1867–1900), professor of Romance languages; fourth from the left is Frank Sumer Earle, professor of biology and horticulture; and on the far right of the second row is Bolling Hall Crenshaw (1867–1935) of the mathematics department.

To the left in the rear row is Emerson R. Miller, professor of pharmacy, and on the right is George Petrie (1866–1947), professor of history and Latin, and additionally the coach of Auburn's first football team.

GROUP OF ALABAMA POLYTECHNIC INSTITUTE PHARMACY STUDENTS AND THEIR PROFESSOR, CIRCA 1899–1900.

Emerson R. Miller (1862–1929) (first row, second from the left) was the first professor of pharmacy at the institute, serving from 1895 to 1905. The pharmacy school's Miller Hall is named in his honor. Peter A. Brannon (back row, second from left) graduated with a degree in pharmacy in 1900. The Williams Collection contains his original diploma.

ABOVE: THE AVONDALE,
ALABAMA, VOLUNTEER FIRE
DEPARTMENT, PHOTOGRAPHED AT
AVONDALE PARK, JULY 1900.

LEFT: STREETCAR ATTACHED
TO THE FAIRVIEW STATION, ENSLEY,
ALABAMA, 1905.

PHOTOGRAPH OF THE ALABAMA
NATIONAL GUARD ENCAMPMENT AT
MONTGOMERY IN AUGUST 1914.

These bandsmen are posed on the steps
of the post office. From the legend it would
appear that they have just or are about to
participate in a parade in honor of Alabama
governor Emmet O'Neal.

PHOTOGRAPH OF THE MOBILE AND
OHIO RAILROAD BASEBALL TEAM
IN 1915.

All but one team member is identified on
the back of the mount. Left to right: Louie
Baumhauer, unidentified, Buck Tacon, Les
Green, Mac McCarron, Maslion Goodman,
Gus Wahl, Luke Tacon, Dave Steber, and John
Donnelly.

ABOVE: LIME COLA BOTTLING
WORKS IN TUSCALOOSA, CIRCA 1916.

The sign reads "5000 Pound of Orange Whistle in One Single Order For Riverview Park. Lime Cola Bottling Works."

RIGHT: THE BOLL WEEVIL MONUMENT IN ENTERPRISE, ALABAMA.

Enterprise was founded in 1882 by John Henry Carmichael, who had moved to that part of Coffee County the previous year. He established a store on what is now North Main Street. With its incorporation in 1896 and the arrival of the Alabama Midland Railroad in 1898, Enterprise experienced rapid growth and became an important cotton producing area, with little diversity.

The Mexican boll weevil invaded the area in 1915 and proceeded to destroy 60 percent of the cotton crop and wreak economic disaster. Local farmers proceeded to diversify their planting but concentrated mainly on peanuts. The move paid dividends, and by 1917 the county led the nation in peanut production.

The citizens of Coffee County expressed their gratitude for their success by erecting the only monument in the world to an agricultural pest. The monument was dedicated in 1919 and is seen as a symbol of the adaptability of mankind to adversity.

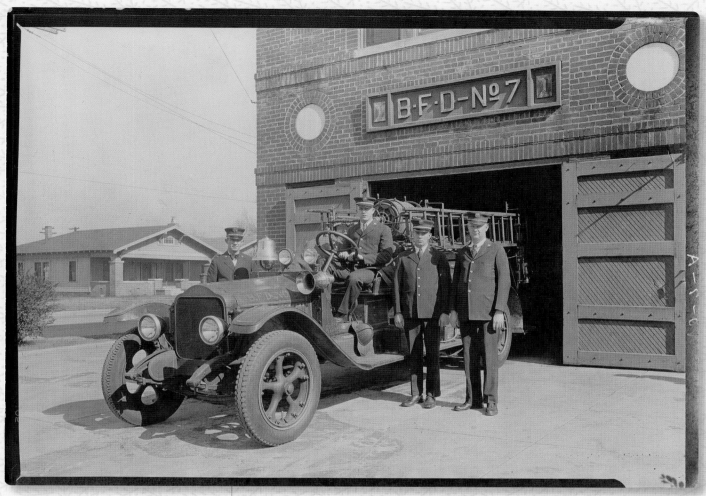

Birmingham Fire Department,
Station Number 7, circa 1920s.

Members of
the Birmingham
Fire Department,
circa 1920s.

**GROUP PHOTOGRAPH
OF THE BIRMINGHAM RIFLE CLUB,
CIRCA 1920S.**

Note the well-dressed young lady in the center, with her weapon slung casually over her arm.

**MISS FANCY, THE ELEPHANT, AND
FRIENDS, TAKEN AT AVONDALE PARK IN
AVONDALE, ALABAMA.**

The area was at the time a separate township; it is now part of Birmingham. The park was founded in the 1880s and soon became a center of community activities. Miss Fancy came to live at the park's city zoo in 1913 and remained there until they abolished the informal zoo in 1934. At that time she was apparently acquired by a circus based in Indiana. Beloved by the children, Miss Fancy was known to join them in the wading pond.

According to one source, the trainer, John Todd, liked to take Miss Fancy on walks down Sixth Avenue and Forty-first Street South. On one occasion Todd had been drinking, and the police decided to take

him to jail. When the officers attempted to return the elephant to the park, Miss Fancy would not budge. After being taunted by the trainer as to how the police were going to get the elephant back to the park, it was decided to set him free.

THE BIRMINGHAM ORANGE-CRUSH
BOTTLING PLANT, CIRCA 1930.

The advertisements on the delivery trucks
say "Ward's Orange-Crush. In the 'Krinkly
Bottle.'" This card was published by the
Birmingham View Company.

EXTERIOR OF THE CURTIS FEED
COMPANY INCORPORATED, MOBILE,
ALABAMA.

Photograph is by the Macer Studio,
Mobile. It would seem quite unlikely that
the company carried anything other than
Purina products.

ABOVE: THE BIRMINGHAM
ELEMENTARY SCHOOLS BOY'S BAND,
CIRCA 1930S. PHOTOGRAPHED BY
OSCAR V. HUNT.

Oscar V. Hunt (1881–1962) was born
in Bowdon, Georgia, but lived most of his
life in Birmingham. Hunt left a brief career
as a streetcar motorman to begin training as
a photographer. He apprenticed with two of
Birmingham's premier early photographers,
Bert Covell and R. T. Boyett. Hunt established his own studio by the early 1920s.
Hunt's body of work included industrial
scenes, streetscapes, and downtown building
construction. Hunt often focused on working people, especially those involved in the
building trades.

RIGHT: THE BIBB COUNTY FOOTBALL
TEAM FOR 1933 PHOTOGRAPHED IN
PIPER, ALABAMA.

RIGHT: DOWNTOWN PRATT CITY, ALABAMA.

The photograph shows Avenue U between Second and Third Streets, circa 1935.

BELOW: HIGHLY DECORATED CARRIAGE, SOMEWHERE IN ALABAMA.

RIGHT: INTERIOR OF A BUILDING HOUSING A BLAST FURNACE AND MOLDING FLOOR FOR HANDLING MOLTEN METAL, SOMEWHERE IN ALABAMA.

The photograph was published by the Philadelphia Museums and has some excellent descriptive text on the reverse of the photographic mount, detailing the use of the blast furnace in making iron.

BELOW: THE J. BLACH AND SONS BUILDING IN DOWNTOWN BIRMINGHAM. PHOTOGRAPHED BY BERT COVELL.

Blach's was founded in 1905 and from then until 1935 was located at Third Avenue and Nineteenth Street. In 1935 it moved into the remodeled Bencor Hotel building on Twentieth Street North shown here. Blach's was known for its high-quality men's clothing and closed its doors in 1987.

BLAST FURNACE AND MOLDING FLOOR
ALABAMA

THE PHILADELPHIA MUSEUMS

ABOVE: POSED PHOTOGRAPH
OF A GROUP OF MINERS.

These African American miners are receiving instruction in treating mine related injuries, notably broken bones. The photograph was taken by R. T. Boyett of Birmingham.

LEFT: PHOTOGRAPH TAKEN AT THE RED MOUNTAIN ORE MINE NUMBER 8 NEAR BIRMINGHAM, ALABAMA.

This mine was part of the Wenonah community of ore mines and was located in the Wenonah Division Camp, which contained five mines. By 1900 all of these mines were being operated by the Tennessee Coal and Iron Company. The Wenonah number 8 mine, originally called the Fossil Mine, was opened in 1887 by the Smith Mining Company.

VII.
THE SOUTH IN FICTION: HISTORY IN A LITERARY CONTEXT

Nelle Harper Lee (1926–) was educated in the Monroeville public schools and then spent one year at Huntington College in Montgomery. From 1945 to 1949 she attended the University of Alabama where she studied law. A year at Oxford University followed and after working in the private sector in the 1950s Lee decided to devote her full time to writing. The result was one of the most famous and influential books ever written by a southerner, winning the Pulitzer Prize in 1961. Its themes of interracial understanding and social justice have caused it to be widely translated.

S TEVE WILLIAMS RECOGnized that the history of a region and culture cannot be told strictly in historical narrative and scholarship. To that end he assembled a collection of authors whose fiction told, in a myriad of ways, the story of the South, southerners, and their history. Every major writer of the period from 1850 to the present is well represented, as well as a number of lesser-known but important authors. The collection is rich in first editions, association copies, and rare books. The Fugitives and the Agrarians, most notably Robert Penn Warren and Allen Tate, are well represented. The collection is supplemented by a small photographic archive as well as correspondence and some manuscript material.

ABOVE:
Original bindings of the two-volume first hardcover printing of Harriet Beecher Stowe's Uncle Tom's Cabin.

TITLE PAGE OF VOLUME ONE OF THE FIRST HARDCOVER PRINTING OF *Uncle Tom's Cabin: or, Life among the Lowly* (BOSTON: JOHN P. JEWETT & COMPANY, 1852).

The author of more than thirty books, Harriet Beecher Stowe (1811–1896) is primarily remembered for this best-selling antislavery novel. It made her an international celebrity and one of the best-known personages of the abolition movement.

Born in Litchfield, Connecticut, to the Reverend Lyman and Roxanna Beecher, Harriet Elisabeth was one of eleven children. All of her seven brothers became ministers, an older sister was a pioneer in women's education, her youngest sister was a major figure in the women's suffrage movement. Harriet had, for the times, an untraditional educational background, it being primarily academic. She pursued writing at an early age, which would allow her the ability to express her beliefs in a world in which women were discouraged from public speaking and could not vote or hold office. In 1832 she met and married Calvin Stowe, a theology professor.

Uncle Tom's Cabin was based on case histories, which Stowe treated in more detail in the *Key to Uncle Tom's Cabin*, published in 1853. She followed this with a second antislavery novel, *Dred*, in 1856. After the Civil War she and her husband established a winter home in Florida to support Stowe's brother Charles Beecher, who had established a school for emancipated African Americans in that state.

UNCLE TOM'S CABIN;

OR,

LIFE AMONG THE LOWLY.

BY

HARRIET BEECHER STOWE.

VOL. I.

THE ADVENTURES

OF

TOM SAWYER

BY

MARK TWAIN.

————————

THE AMERICAN PUBLISHING COMPANY,
HARTFORD, CONN.: CHICAGO, ILL.: CINCINNATI, OHIO.
A. ROMAN & CO., SAN FRANCISCO, CAL.
1876.

BELOW: *Original binding of* The Adventures of Tom Sawyer.

FIRST EDITION OF MARK TWAIN'S
THE ADVENTURES OF TOM SAWYER
(HARTFORD, CT: THE AMERICAN
PUBLISHING COMPANY, 1876).

Samuel Langhorne Clemens (1835–1910), better known by his pen name Mark Twain, was born in Florida, Missouri, and his family moved to Hannibal in 1839. After an early career as a printer, he learned steamboat piloting, and from 1857 to 1861 he traveled the Mississippi River. During these years he observed and absorbed much relating to life in the river towns and in slave-holding society in general.

After a brief (and later comically related) stint in the Confederate army, Clemens went to Nevada and then to San Francisco, where he pursued a journalism career. To say that he mastered the extravagant forms of satire and hoax that prevailed in the journalism of that period would be an understatement.

Materials from his southern roots and personal reminiscences figure prominently in some of his best work, including *The Adventures of Tom Sawyer* (1876), *Life on the Mississippi* (1883), *Adventures of Huckleberry Finn* (1885) and *Pudd'nhead Wilson* (1894).

The great popularity of his books brought him fortune, but poor investments left him broke at the age of sixty.

Twain spent his latter years rebuilding his finances, and though he published a number of books, his best work was behind him. His wife and all of his children save his daughter Clara predeceased him.

ORIGINAL BINDING OF CHARLES W. CHESNUTT'S FIRST BOOK, *THE CONJURE WOMAN* (BOSTON: HOUGHTON, MIFFLIN AND COMPANY, 1899).

Charles W. Chesnutt (1858–1932) was born in Ohio but spent his formative years in the area around Fayetteville, North Carolina, where his family roots were very deep. Chesnutt was extremely light-skinned and could have easily passed for white but determined to live his life as a black man. After a stint as a schoolteacher and principal in North Carolina, he moved to New York City in 1883 to establish himself as a stenographer. Moving from there to Cleveland, Ohio, where he would spend the rest of his life, he became an involved citizen and activist. Chesnutt was on Booker T. Washington's Committee of Twelve and the General Committee of the NAACP, as well as in numerous local civic and cultural organizations.

BABY PICTURE OF TRUMAN CAPOTE AT AGE SEVEN MONTHS.

Truman Capote (1924–1984) was named Truman Streckfus Persons at his birth in New Orleans. After divorcing his father, his mother later married Joseph Garcia Capote. Truman Capote was four years old when that marriage ended, and he spent the

Chesnutt's interest in southern folklore is evidenced by the stories in *The Conjure Woman,* which was written in dialect, as was accepted practice at the time in southern literature. These and other stories in his second book, *The Wife of His Youth* (1899), are complex and sharply drawn, dealing with such themes as mixed race, African Americans "passing" as white, illegitimacy, and social mores between blacks and whites.

Chesnutt pursued these themes and others in three later novels and also published a well-received biography of Frederick Douglass. In 1928 he was awarded the Spingarn Medal by the NAACP.

next six years living with relatives in Monroeville, Alabama. His friends during this period were Edwin and Harper Lee, author of *To Kill a Mockingbird.* Reunited with his mother in 1935, Capote continued his education at schools in New York and Connecticut.

His first novel, *Other Voices, Other Rooms,* published in 1948, reflects Capote's childhood sense of isolation and insecurity. His best-known works are perhaps *Breakfast at Tiffany's,* published in 1958, and his "nonfiction novel" *In Cold Blood.* Published in 1959 after five years of research, it chronicled the murder of the Clutter family of Holcomb, Kansas. The Williams Collection contains many of Capote's works in first edition.

DUST JACKET FOR WILLIAM FAULKNER'S
THIRD BOOK, *MOSQUITOES* (NEW YORK:
BONI AND LIVERIGHT, 1927).

William Cuthbert Faulkner (1897–1962), one of the greatest American novelists, was born in New Albany, Mississippi, but spent the majority of his childhood in Oxford in that state. His great-grandfather William Clark Falkner was a Confederate soldier and as its colonel commanded the Second Mississippi Infantry at the Battle of First Manassas in July of 1861. He later raised the Seventh Mississippi Cavalry and served as its colonel. Colonel Falkner was assassinated in 1889.

Though a bright student, Faulkner eventually dropped out of high school and soon after quit his job at his grandfather's bank to pursue the writing of poetry. His first book, *The Marble Faun* (1924), was a collection of verse financed by himself and a longtime friend. *Soldier's Pay* (1925), a novel about the disillusionment of the post–World War I generation, followed soon after. *Mosquitoes*, a satiric look at the New Orleans artistic community of the mid-1920s, appeared in 1927.

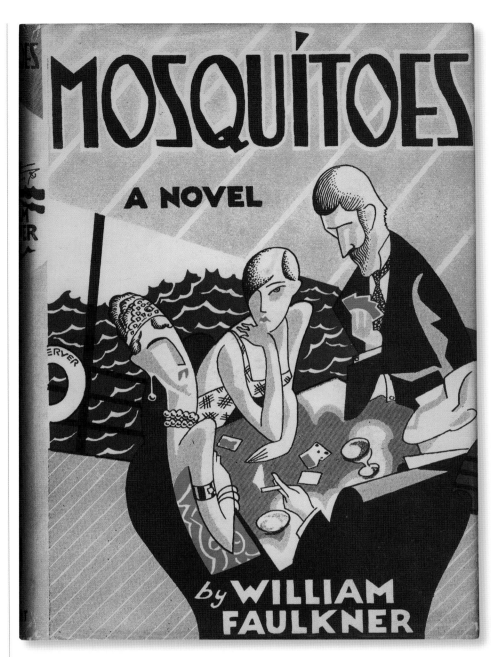

In 1929 Faulkner published both *Sartoris* and *The Sound and the Fury*, but the 1930s was his most productive decade, seeing the appearance of *As I Lay Dying* (1930), *Sanctuary* (1931), *These 13* (1931), *Light in August* (1932), *Pylon (1935), Absalom! Absalom!* (1936), *The Unvanquished* (1938), and *The Wild Palms (1939)*. Faulkner was awarded the Nobel Prize for Literature in 1950. The Williams Collection contains a number of Faulkner's works in the first edition, and it also holds Eudora Welty's copy of *These 13*.

Dust jacket of Zelda Fitzgerald's only book, *Save Me the Waltz* (New York: Scribner, 1932).

Zelda Sayre (1900–1948), who epitomized the "flapper" of the so-called "lost generation" of 1920s America, was born in Montgomery, Alabama. Her father, Anthony Dickson Sayre, was an Alabama Supreme Court justice, and her mother, the former Minnie Buckner Machen, was the daughter of a Confederate senator. Zelda was a prominent belle in World War I–era Montgomery, and while attending a dance just after her high school graduation in 1918, she met F. Scott Fitzgerald, then an army officer at a nearby training camp.

Scott pursued her for almost two years, with her finally agreeing to marriage in 1920 after the acceptance for publication of his first novel,

This Side of Paradise. The book, noted for its vivid portrayal of the excesses of the "lost generation," created a firestorm of publicity for the couple, and Zelda was frequently quoted for her opinion on women's issues of the day. Her influence on his later novels is frequently noted, and her personality and experiences flavor virtually all of his writings. The breakdown of their marriage in the late 1920s coincided with the beginning of her many hospitalizations for mental illness.

Save Me the Waltz, a fictionalized account of her stormy marriage, is her only published novel. F. Scott Fitzgerald deeply resented the book and maintained the position that she had utilized portions of his plot for *Tender Is the Night* in its writing. The book garnered little favorable comment and sold very poorly.

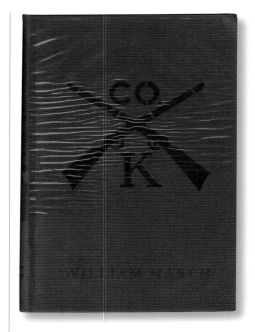

Original binding of William March's *Company K* (New York: H. Smith & R. Haas, 1933), with a portion of its original transparent glassine dust wrapper.

William March (1893–1954), a native of Mobile, spent a year studying law at the University of Alabama in 1915. Unable to continue because of financial difficulties, he secured work in New York as a law clerk. March joined the US Marine Corps in 1917, and his military exploits in France earned him both the Navy Cross (that service's second highest award behind the Medal of Honor) and the Distinguished Service Cross. After the war he commenced a very successful business career. He retired to pursue a writing career in 1938.

Company K, his first novel, is based on his war experiences but achieved little commercial or critical success. His novels and stories have varied backgrounds but reflect his poverty-ridden upbringing in rural Alabama. They chronicle the conflicts spawned by class division, racial inequality, and family. His last novel, *The Bad Seed* (1954), became a best seller, but March did not live to see its success. The novel was eventually turned into a stage play and a movie.

SAVE ME THE WALTZ

ZELDA FITZGERALD

Dust jacket of the first edition of Carson McCullers' first novel, *The Heart Is a Lonely Hunter* (Boston: Houghton Mifflin, 1940).

Carson McCullers (1917–1967) was born Lula Carson Smith in Columbus, Georgia. A product of a middle-class upbringing, her childhood was filled with a sense of southern heritage and traditions, including stories of family members who had fought in the Civil War. McCullers studied creative writing at Columbia University and made a concerted effort to live outside the South. Plagued by ill health for most of her life she returned periodically to Columbus to recuperate and there met and married James Reeves McCullers Jr., an aspiring writer. McCullers finished *The Heart Is a Lonely Hunter* in 1939 and finished her second, *Reflections in a Golden Eye,* in just two months. In addition to her novels she published a number of short stories and nonfiction prose pieces.

Dust jacket to the first edition of Eudora Welty's collection of short stories, *The Wide Net and Other Stories* (New York: Harcourt, Brace and Company, 1943).

Eudora Welty (1909–2001) was born in Jackson, Mississippi, and with brief exceptions lived her entire life there. Her childhood reading included "fairy tales, legends and Mississippi history" according to one source. Her father, an avid photographer, encouraged her interest in that genre. Welty spent several years at Mississippi State College for Women and later transferred to the University of Wisconsin where she received a BA in 1929.

The Depression-era job market forced her return to Jackson where she worked from 1933 to 1936 for the Works Progress Administration. Welty traveled the state, doing feature stories, taking photographs, and interacting with her fellow Mississippians, black and white. Welty at this time began pursuing short story writing, using the observations and materials gathered in her WPA work. One of her published stories attracted the attention of Robert Penn Warren and Cleanth Brooks, editors of *the Southern Review*, who began publishing other stories.

Books of short stories and novels followed, and Welty became one of the most prolific and well-known southern authors. She was elected to the American Academy of Arts and Letters in 1971, and her novel *The Optimist's Daughter* won the Pulitzer Prize in 1973. The Williams Collections contains a large group of first editions of her prose as well as a number of her photographs.

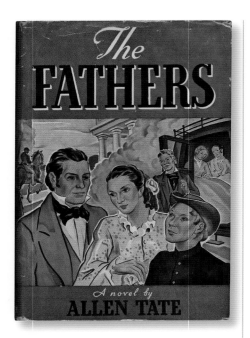

Dust jacket of the first edition of Allen Tate's *The Fathers* (New York: G. P. Putnam's Sons, 1938).

Allen John Orley Tate (1899–1979), novelist, essayist, and poet, was born in Winchester, Kentucky. He attended Vanderbilt University in 1918, studying writing under John Crowe Ransom. He joined Ransom, Donald Davidson, and other writers in founding the literary magazine the *Fugitive* in 1922, and he became a member of the Fugitive movement.

In 1924 he married the novelist Caroline Gordon, and his first book, *Mr. Pope and Other Poems,* appeared in 1928. In 1930, Tate—along with former Fugitives Ransom, Davidson, and Robert Penn Warren, formed the Agrarian group—and published the influential and controversial *I'll Take My Stand.* Featuring twelve essayists, it praised, on a cultural level, the superiority of the agricultural economy of the South over the industrialization of the North.

The Fathers is a historical novel set in the opening days of the Civil War in Virginia and is very much steeped in Southern tradition of that period. The Williams Collection has a substantial number of Tate's works, including a copy of *I'll Take My Stand.*

Letter from Walker Percy, dated August 18, 1977, to Walter Sullivan saying he will write a letter on behalf of Allen Tate in support of his nomination for the Nobel Prize for literature.

Walter Sullivan (1924–2006) was professor of English at Vanderbilt University and later chancellor of the Fellowship of Southern Writers.

Dear Walter—

Yours is the address I have, so I'll write you in answer to kind inquiry by messrs McDowell, Sullivan and Cheney re: Allen Tate for the Nobel. Although (1) I've no idea that the Nobel Committee pays any attention to letters and (2) least of all mine, (3) I most heartily endorse your sentiments about Allen and (4) shall accordingly write to Nobel Committee.

Cordially
—Walker

(my C.B. handle, should you be in these parts: Dr Doolittle, duck hunter—up)

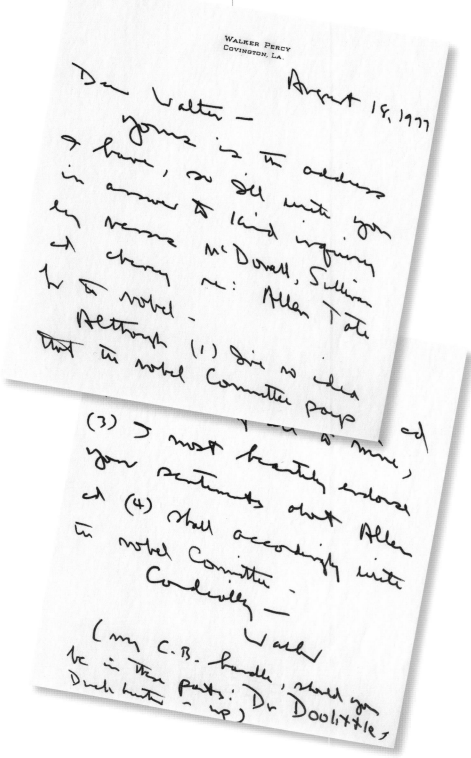

poems in 1935; prior to that he had written a nonfiction life of John Brown.

From 1934 to 1942 Warren taught at Louisiana State University, where he founded the *Southern Review*. His prolific prose and poetry output resulted in his holding the honor of being the only American writer to win a Pulitzer Prize for both fiction and poetry. His volume of poems *Promises* won the Pulitzer in 1958. The Williams Collection has an extremely important Warren collection, comprising all his major works in first edition as well as numerous periodical contributions and a small photographic archive.

DUST JACKET OF THE FIRST EDITION OF ROBERT PENN WARREN'S PULITZER PRIZE–WINNING NOVEL *ALL THE KING'S MEN* (NEW YORK: HARCOURT, BRACE, 1946).

Robert Penn Warren (1905–1989), one of the Vanderbilt University group that launched the Fugitive and the Agrarian movements, was born in Guthrie, Kentucky. He was educated in public schools there and in Clarksville, Tennessee. Warren went to Vanderbilt to study chemistry, but with Allen Tate as a roommate, he soon began to consider writing. Joining the Fugitive group with Tate, John Crowe Ransom, and Donald Davidson, he published his first volume of

Walker Percy (1916–1990) occupies perhaps a unique place in southern literature. Orphaned as a teenager, he went to live in Greenville, Mississippi, with his father's cousin, William Alexander Percy, author of *Lanterns on the Levee: Recollections of a Planter's Son* (1941). There Percy was exposed to the southern literary life by numerous visiting writers. At his "Uncle Will's" request Percy studied medicine at Columbia University, and while working at a clinic in Greenville, he contracted pulmonary tuberculosis. While recovering, he read widely in existentialist philosophy and began a serious study of language as the medium that defines the human condition. Percy's scientific background and personal philosophy introduced into his writing a disdain for the treating of human existence in narrow avenues dictated by an increasingly regimented culture.

The Moviegoer, Percy's first novel, chronicles the story of John Binkerson "Binx" Bolling, a young stockbroker in 1950s New Orleans. Bolling is struggling with issues of self identity, complicated by family matters, the perceived decline of southern traditions, and traumatic experiences in the Korean War. This novel, like the balance of Percy's work, is heavily influenced by the existential. However, Percy treats it with a lighter tone than many authors. *The Moviegoer* won the National Book Award for fiction in 1962 and has been included on several lists of the top one hundred English language novels of the twentieth century.

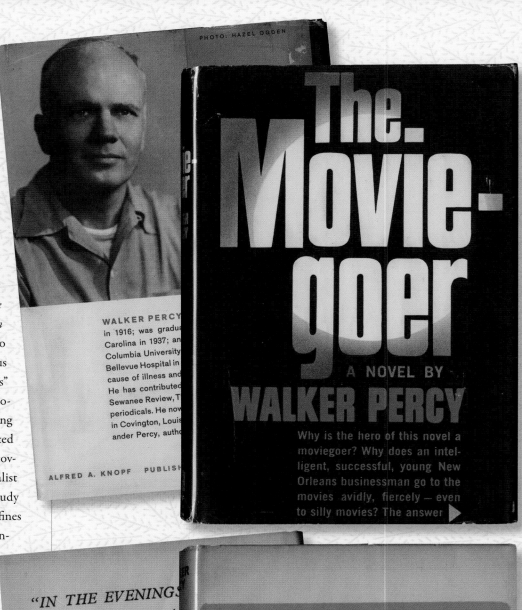

Signed carbon copy of the option for assignment of the movie rights for The Moviegoer.

OPTION

By this agreement, executed as of this 30th day of July, 1962, WALKER PERCY (hereinafter referred to as the "Owner") and RANSDELL COX (hereinafter referred to as the "Purchaser") agree as follows:

1. The Owner hereby grants the Purchaser an option (hereinafter referred to as the "Option") to purchase certain rights in the novel entitled "THE MOVIEGOER", which rights are more particularly described in a written Purchase Agreement being executed between the parties simultaneously with the execution of this agreement but which shall be dated and deemed delivered as of the date the Option is exercised.

2. As consideration for the Option, the Purchaser shall, simultaneously with the execution of this agreement, pay the Owner FIVE HUNDRED DOLLARS ($500.00), which shall be applicable against the cash purchase price as defined in Paragraph ELEVENTH of the Purchase Agreement attached hereto, said payment to be made by check payable to Annie Laurie Williams, Inc., as agent.

3. The Purchaser may exercise the Option by giving the Owner written notice in accordance with Paragraph FIFTEENTH of the Purchase Agreement, and by simultaneously therewith making the payment required by Paragraph ELEVENTH of the Purchase Agreement, such notice to be given and such payment to be made not later than three (3) months after the date of this Option.

4. The Purchaser shall have the right to extend the Option for an additional period of three (3) months by giving the Owner written notice on or before the termination of the original three (3) months period, and by simultaneously therewith paying the Owner an additional sum of FIVE HUNDRED DOLLARS ($500.00), by check payable to the aforesaid agent, which sum shall also be applicable against the aforementioned cash purchase price. In the event the Purchaser elects so to extend the Option, the Purchaser may exercise the Option in the manner herein set forth at any time within six (6) months from the date hereof.

...ice is not given and such payment is not made ...months period, this contract shall be of no ...fect. Owner shall in any event be entitled to ...t forth in Articles 2 and 4 above.

...that the Purchaser shall exercise his Option, ...in thirty (30) days after the exercise thereof, ...r cause the execution and delivery by others, ...rt form assignment by the Owner to the Pur- ...standard form, for recording in the Office ...yrights, and such additional documents as ...quired by the Purchaser fully to convey to ...otion picture, television and allied rights

...shall be binding upon and shall inure to ...es hereto and their respective heirs, per- ...uccessors and assigns, and is assignable ...d the assignee shall assume all of the ...hereunder.

...nd any agreements executed by the parties ...ith constitute the entire agreement between the parties and cannot be modified except by a written instrument executed by the parties hereto.

IN WITNESS WHEREOF, the parties have executed this agreement as of the day and year first above written.

WALKER PERCY

RANSDELL COX

- 2 -

PHOTOGRAPHIC ALBUM RELATING TO
THE LINCOLN NORMAL SCHOOL IN
MARION, ALABAMA.

The Williams Collection has two albums
of photographs relating to the Lincoln Normal School, chartered in 1868. The school
closed in 1970 after a century of educating
African American school children.

VIII.
A PROUD
HERITAGE: THE
AFRICAN AMERICAN
EXPERIENCE IN ALABAMA
AND THE SOUTH

Photographs

A Class - Second Grade - 1922

1922

B Class - Second Grade - 1922

Norman

Paul Patton - 1922

THE AFRICAN AMERICAN experience in Alabama is well represented in the A. S. Williams III Americana Collection through extensive holdings in the book and pamphlet collection. The Williams Collection also holds an important body of work by a noted African American artist as well as numerous photographs reflecting the lives of blacks in Alabama and across the South. Steve Williams made a special effort to collect significant material on Booker T. Washington, George Washington Carver, and the Tuskegee Institute. Despite the scarcity of such material, the Williams Collection has assembled an archive of importance in this area.

The collection also holds an interesting and important archive created by Jennie C. Lee, choir director at Tuskegee from 1903 to 1928. A smaller but important group of materials relates to Ephraim Madison Henry, a Tuskegee choir member under William L. Dawson, who headed the choir from 1931 to 1955. Henry received the bachelor of science degree in education in 1934.

ORIGINAL BINDING OF GEORGE W. WILLIAMS'S *A HISTORY OF THE NEGRO TROOPS IN THE WAR OF THE REBELLION, 1861–1865, PRECEDED BY A REVIEW OF THE MILITARY SERVICES OF NEGROES IN ANCIENT AND MODERN TIMES* (NEW YORK: HARPER & BROTHERS, 1888).

George Washington Williams (1849–1891) was a native of Pennsylvania and joined the Union army at the age of fourteen, enlisting under a false name and serving until the end of the war. It would appear he went to Mexico at the end of war to join the forces fighting against the Emperor Maximilian.

Returning to the United States, he reenlisted in the US Army but served only a year.

Following an interest in the ministry he was admitted to Newton Theological Institute in 1870, becoming the first African American graduate in 1874. Ordained as a Baptist minister, he held several pastorates, including that of the Twelfth Baptist Church of Boston. He moved to a pastorate in Cincinnati in 1876 and entered politics there, becoming the first African American elected to the Ohio legislature.

Williams's career as a historian resulted in his highly regarded *History of the Negro Race in America from 1619 to 1880: Negroes as Slaves, as Soldiers and as Citizens*, published in 1883.

Traveling in Europe, Williams made the acquaintance of King Leopold of Belgium and through him took an interest in the Belgian colonies in Africa, notably the Congo. A visit there caused Williams to write several famous articles on the poor treatment of the people of that country, leading to an international outcry.

CARTE DE VISITE, CIRCA 1867–1870, SHOWING WHAT APPEARS TO BE AFRICAN AMERICAN FOOD VENDORS AT A RAILROAD SIDING SOMEWHERE IN ALABAMA.

The image was taken by J. F. Stanton's Photograph Gallery, which was located at 49 Dauphin Street, Mobile.

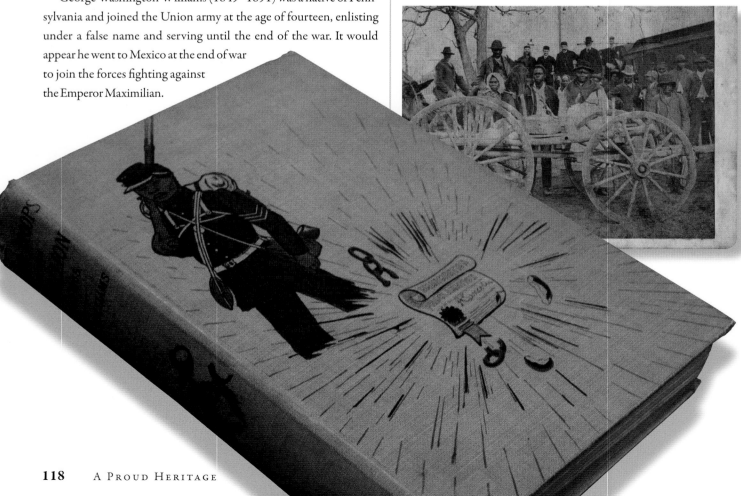

The State of Ala.

Russell County. Articles of agreement made the 30

ecember 1865 — between P. H. Perry of the above State & County

the first part; & Peter former slave of P. H. Perry of the 2ma part

which of the Second part agrees for himself to work during

[the] Next year faithfully & Not drink or leave the premises with

[consent] presenting the first part & be accountable obeying all orders

of the first part & be accountable to damage to loss of put in

his care — that may occur by neglect — and to assist to get

timber or other work about the wood shop that is absolutely

Necessary — first part paying 2ninty five cents for day — & to

Commence work early in the morning — & Not stop for breakfast

More than Twenty minutes at any time — & Not more than

one hour until the first day of april — & Not more than

one hour & a half until the 1st day of June & Not more than

Than two hours the ballance of the Summer, & Not more

[first] part further agrees to direct one dollar per day for all loss

by sickness or other causes, Pay all Drs Bills & Clothing, &

one for Shoes — that first agrees to furnish wife of 2nma

[?] ma 10 lbs of Cotton & One pair shoes —

agrees for his wife to do all plantation work do

first part — the first part agrees to furnish

Soon — & 6½ lbs of Meat to furn self wife & cl

Meal — this entered to Commce the 1st a

And ma the 25th day of Decr 1866 each

of this Contract Signed in the [?]

First part agrees to furnish tools &

[agreement with Peter slave(?) endorsed by freedmens Bureau]

ARTICLES OF AGREEMENT
DATED DECEMBER OF 1865
BETWEEN P. H. PERRY OF
RUSSELL COUNTY, ALABAMA,
AND PETER, HIS FORMER SLAVE.

   The agreement was to begin on January 1, 1866, and remain in force until
December 25 of that year. The agreement sets
forth Perry's expectations of Peter in terms of
his duties and establishes his daily break periods
and pay. The contract was formally approved by
J. F. Waddell, an agent for the Freedmen's Bureau.

DEPOSIT BOOK OF THE NATIONAL
FREEDMEN'S SAVINGS AND TRUST
COMPANY. ISSUED BY THE BRANCH IN
HUNTSVILLE, ALABAMA, IT BELONGED
TO ONE BASSELL PICKETT AND
DOCUMENTS HIS TRANSACTIONS
FROM 1868 TO 1883.

Also known as the Freedmen's Saving
Bank, this organization was created by the
US government to assist newly emancipated
African Americans in developing a relationship with a financial institution. An arm of
the Freedmen's Bureau, its charter was signed
into law by Abraham Lincoln in March of
1865. By 1866 it had nineteen branches in
twelve states.

In the beginning it was anticipated that
the bank would primarily be a repository
for African American veterans, ex-slaves,
and their families. As the concept gained
wider acceptance, churches and charitable
societies also opened accounts and trusts
with the bank.

The Panic of 1873 along with some
unsound management decisions led to the
bank's failure in 1874. Congress established
a program to reimburse depositors, but many
were never compensated. The Huntsville
branch may have carried on in some fashion,
as Bassell Pickett made deposit entries from
1875 to 1883, although these entries may
reflect activities with another institution.

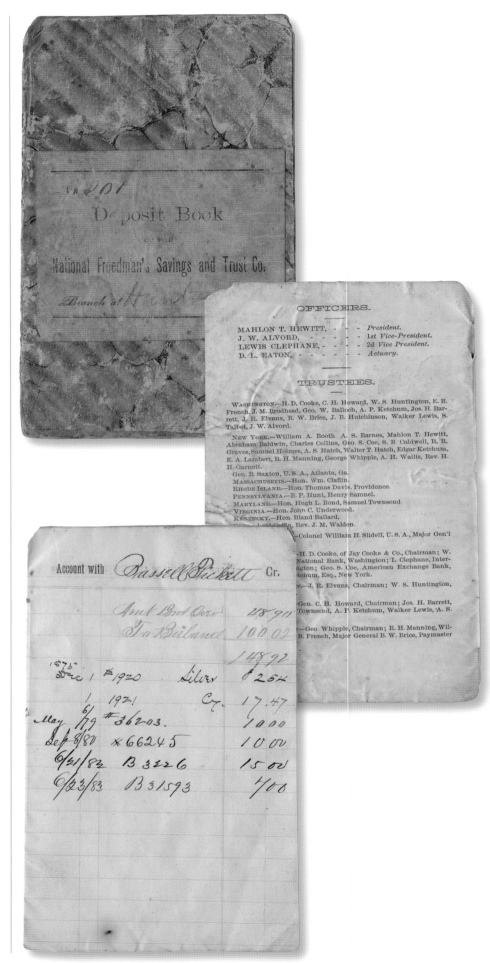

THREE STEREOVIEWS OF AFRICAN
AMERICAN TROOPS TRAINING FOR
SERVICE IN WORLD WAR I.
  The Williams Collection holds a large
number of stereoviews related to African
Americans.

Front cover and title page of Booker T. Washington's *Daily Resolves* (London: Ernest Nister; New York: E. P. Dutton & Co., 1896).

The front cover displays the notation "Gem Series." The leaves are unpaginated.

Front cover and title page of a rare first edition of Booker T. Washington's *Black-Belt Diamonds: Gems from the Speeches, Addresses and Talks to Students of Booker T. Washington* (New York: Fortune & Scott, Publishers, 1898).

This collection was "selected and arranged" by Victoria Earle Matthews, with an introduction by T. Thomas Fortune, a prominent African American journalist, author, and publisher.

BLACK-BELT DIAMONDS

Gems from the Speeches, Addresses, and Talks to Students

OF

BOOKER T. WASHINGTON

Principal of Tuskegee Institute, Tuskegee, Ala.

Selected and Arranged by

VICTORIA EARLE MATTHEWS

AUTHOR OF "AUNT LINDY," ETC.

INTRODUCTION

BY T. THOMAS FORTUNE

NEW YORK
FORTUNE AND SCOTT, PUBLISHERS
4 CEDAR STREET
1898

Booker T. Washington's *Putting the Most into Life* (New York: Thomas Y. Crowell Company, 1906). One of several inspirational volumes from Washington, this volume identifies Washington as the author of *Up from Slavery*, perhaps his most famous work.

Booker Taliaferro Washington (1856–1915) was born into slavery in his native Virginia. After a secondary education at Hampton Institute in Hampton, Virginia, and a brief career as a teacher, he accepted a teaching position at his alma mater.

The Tuskegee Normal School for Colored Teachers was founded in July of 1881, making it the second oldest historically black college in Alabama. The bill passed in the legislature was woefully underfunded—there being no monies allocated for facilities. The search for a principal resulted in Washington's accepting the position.

Under his guidance Tuskegee became a leader in creating a curriculum leaning heavily toward industrial education and

Washington became its primary advocate. This position helped attract white philanthropists such as Julius Rosenwald and Andrew Carnegie but alienated black intellectuals such as W. E. B. DuBois, who were advocating a liberal arts education for African American students.

Washington's efforts at fundraising were so successful that Tuskegee became a private entity in 1892, although the state continued its status as a land-grant college. With Tuskegee's growth Washington was able to attract faculty members of prominence, including George Washington Carver.

With Washington's death in 1915, the industrial education model lost its preeminent spokesman. His successor, Robert Russa Moton, a former administrator at Hampton Institute, began the establishment of a liberal arts curriculum and a de-emphasis of Washington's original vision.

*Original binding of
Washington's* Putting the Most into Life.

*Title page of
Washington's* Putting the Most into Life.

EXAMPLES OF BOOKER T. WASHINGTON'S
INDUSTRIAL EDUCATION CONCEPTS.

Right: John Charles Jordan's *The Art
of Making Harness Successfully* (Tuskegee:
Institute Press, 1913). Jordan was head of
the Division of Harness Making and Carriage Trimming.

Below right: Frank L. West's *How to Repair Shoes* (Tuskegee: Institute Press, 1912).
West was head of the Shoemaking Division.

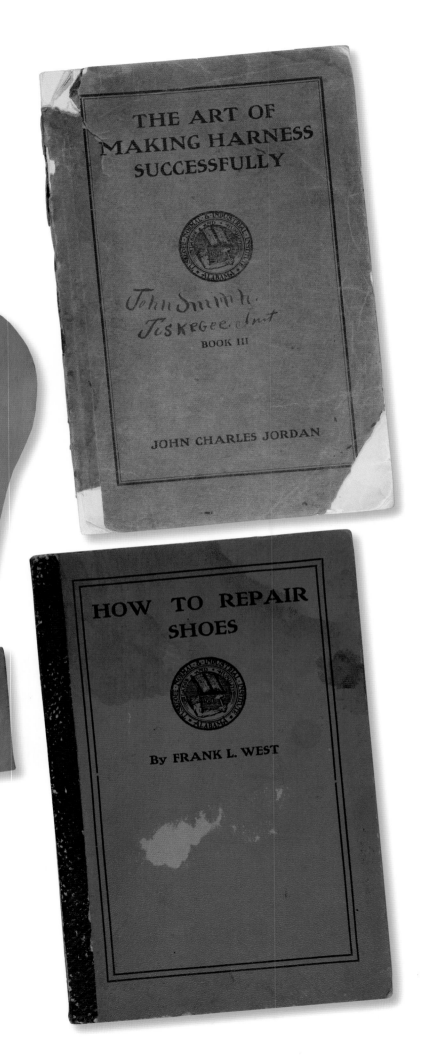

These patterns were folded into Jordan's
The Art of Making Harness Successfully.

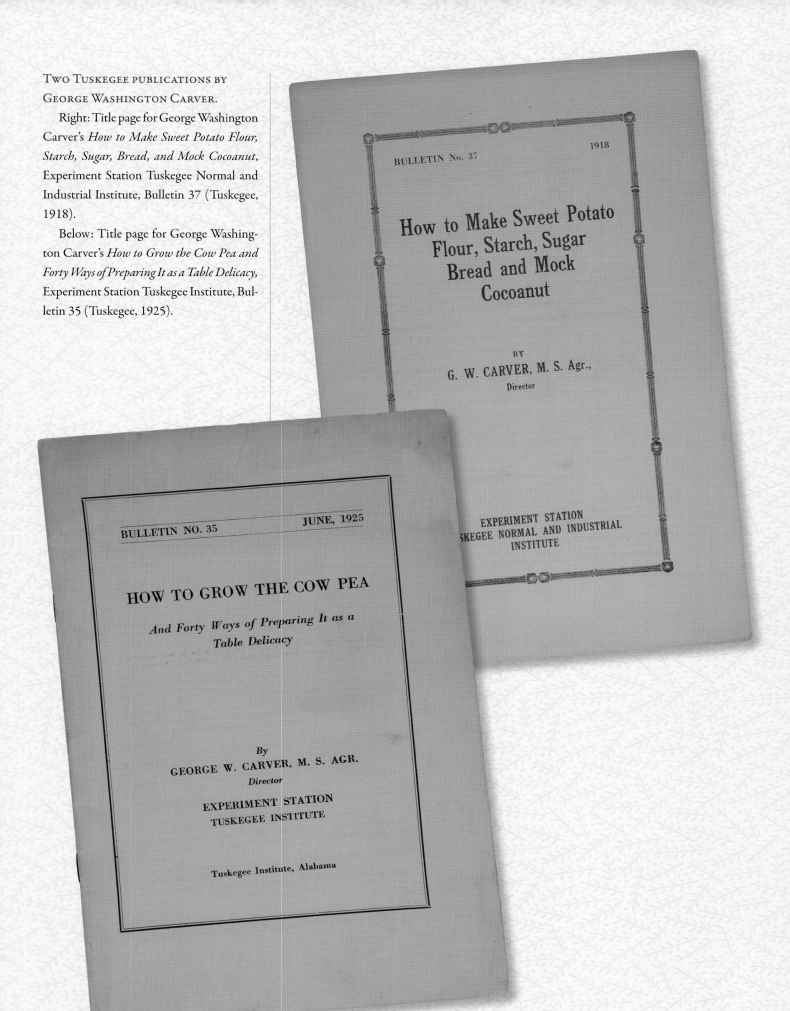

TWO TUSKEGEE PUBLICATIONS BY GEORGE WASHINGTON CARVER.

Right: Title page for George Washington Carver's *How to Make Sweet Potato Flour, Starch, Sugar, Bread, and Mock Cocoanut,* Experiment Station Tuskegee Normal and Industrial Institute, Bulletin 37 (Tuskegee, 1918).

Below: Title page for George Washington Carver's *How to Grow the Cow Pea and Forty Ways of Preparing It as a Table Delicacy,* Experiment Station Tuskegee Institute, Bulletin 35 (Tuskegee, 1925).

BULLETIN No. 37   1918

How to Make Sweet Potato Flour, Starch, Sugar Bread and Mock Cocoanut

BY

G. W. CARVER, M. S. Agr.,

Director

EXPERIMENT STATION
TUSKEGEE NORMAL AND INDUSTRIAL
INSTITUTE

BULLETIN NO. 35   JUNE, 1925

HOW TO GROW THE COW PEA

And Forty Ways of Preparing It as a
Table Delicacy

By

GEORGE W. CARVER, M. S. AGR.

Director

EXPERIMENT STATION
TUSKEGEE INSTITUTE

Tuskegee Institute, Alabama

PHOTOGRAPH OF JENNIE C. LEE,
CHOIR DIRECTOR OF THE TUSKEGEE
INSTITUTE FROM 1903 TO 1928.

Jennie Cheatham Lee was a graduate
of the music program at Fisk University in
Nashville. A pupil of Jennie A. Robinson,
the first head of Fisk's music department, she
came to Tuskegee in 1903 to serve as choir
director. She brought with her as assistants
two fellow students, Willa Hadley and Mi-
randa Waters.

Music had been a part of the
culture of Tuskegee almost from
the beginning. Washington
formed the Tuskegee Quartet
in 1884 as an outreach arm of
the institute, and the school choir
dates from 1886. The choir was
originally established to perform
for vespers and special occasions.

William L. Dawson, who headed the choir from 1931 to 1955
and took it to international fame,
learned to read music from Lee
while a student at Tuskegee.

RIGHT: A 1928 LETTER FROM
ROBERT R. MOTON, THEN
PRESIDENT OF TUSKEGEE, TO
JENNIE C. LEE REGARDING HER
RETIREMENT.

Tuskegee Normal & Industrial Institute
BOOKER T. WASHINGTON, PRINCIPAL
TUSKEGEE INSTITUTE, ALABAMA.

April 10, 1906.

Mrs. J. C. Lee:-

I beg to thank you for your helpful part in making the
exercises during the Anniversary so helpful and satisfactory.
In this formal way I wish you to know how deeply indebted the
school is to you for what you have done.

I am sure you must have been gratified, as all of us were,
with the high compliment which Mr. Carnegie paid your choir.
Such praise is not often given to a choir or any musical organization.

Principal.

H.

TUSKEGEE INSTITUTE, ALABAMA
ROBERT R. MOTON

May 19th
1928

My dear Mrs. Lee:

The trustees having accepted
your resignation and placed your name on the
retired list, I am writing to express on behalf
of faculty, students, alumni and friends our
heartfelt appreciation of the really distinguished service which you have rendered the Institute and through it the cause of Negro education
and particularly of Negro folk-music, through
the twenty-five years of your unbroken connection
with the school.

Your conscientious, painstaking,
efficient labors have set a standard of artistic
achievement that few in this field can equal and
none surpass, a goal worthy of the best efforts
of any who may come after you.

We want you to carry with you
the assurance of our continued admiration and es-
teem, as well as our abiding affection. And I
trust that you will return to us as often as
your inclination and convenience may prompt, know-
ing that always a sincere and cordial welcome a-
waits you without previous invitation or notice.

Sincerely yours,

Mrs. Jennie C. Lee,
Tuskegee Institute,
Alabama.   Principal.

ABOVE: LETTER FROM
BOOKER T. WASHINGTON
TO JENNIE C. LEE DATED
APRIL 1906.

Washington thanks Lee
for the part played by the
choir in the twenty-fifth anniversary celebration of the
founding of the Tuskegee
Institute. Washington notes
that Andrew Carnegie was
most complimentary of
the choir's performance.

Programs from the Ephraim M. Henry archive, documenting performances by the Tuskegee Institute Choir as well as visiting musical artists.

Right: Program for Negro Spirituals, a concert given by the Tuskegee Institute Choir and Men's Chorus at Denny Stadium.

Below: Program for a concert featuring Marian Anderson accompanied by William King held at the Tuskegee Institute Chapel on March 11, 1931.

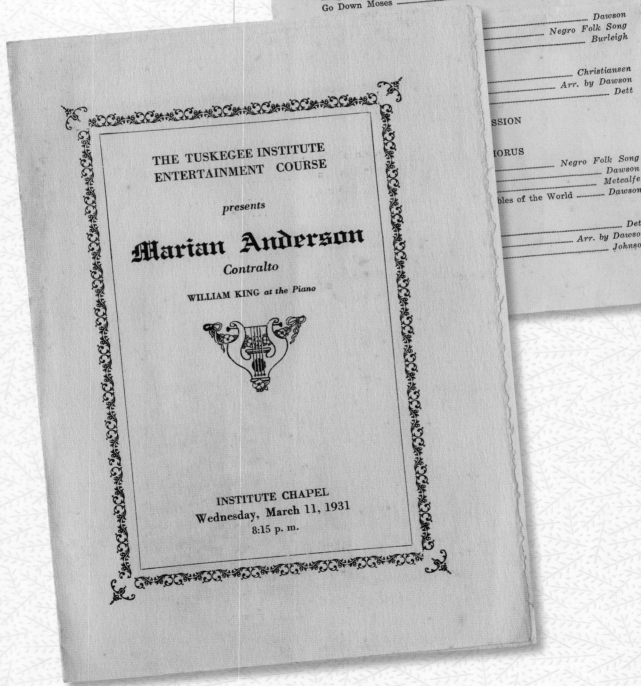

THE
TUSKEGEE INSTITUTE CHOIR
AND MEN'S CHORUS
in
Negro Spirituals
WILLIAM L. DAWSON, CONDUCTOR
DENNY STADIUM
Saturday, May 14th—8:00 p. m.
————
PROGRAMME

I

Steal Away	Arr. by Dawson
	Dawson
King Jesus is a Listenin'	Arr. by Burleigh
Go Down Moses	
	Dawson
	Negro Folk Song
	Burleigh
	Christiansen
	Arr. by Dawson
	Dett

...SSION

...HORUS

	Negro Folk Song
	Dawson
	Metcalfe
...bles of the World	Dawson
	Dett
	Arr. by Dawson
	Johnson

THE TUSKEGEE INSTITUTE
ENTERTAINMENT COURSE

presents

Marian Anderson
Contralto

WILLIAM KING at the Piano

INSTITUTE CHAPEL
Wednesday, March 11, 1931
8:15 p. m.

PROGRAM FOR THE TUSKEGEE
INSTITUTE CHOIR'S 1932
PERFORMANCE AT RADIO CITY
MUSIC HALL.

Ephraim M. Henry participated as a choir
member in the 1932 performance at Radio
City Music Hall. Performances such as these
gave national recognition to the institute's
music program as well as to William L.
Dawson, the choir's talented composer and
director.

William Levi Dawson (1899–1990) was
born in Anniston, Alabama, and at the age
of thirteen ran away from home to attend
the Tuskegee Institute. He was a member
of the band and the orchestra, and left the
school in 1921.

He furthered his musical education in
Kansas and Chicago, and held the position
of first trombonist in the Chicago Civic Orchestra from 1926 to 1930, winning several
awards during that period.

Dawson returned to Tuskegee as musical
director in 1931 and stayed until his retirement in 1955. During his tenure the choir
performed for Presidents Herbert Hoover
and Franklin Delano Roosevelt, and in
such illustrious venues as Carnegie Hall,
the Academy of Music at Philadelphia, and
Constitution Hall. Dawson was a highly
regarded compos-
er, his *Negro Folk
Symphony* being his
best-known work.
Dawson received the
coveted Tuskegee
University Board of
Trustees Distinguish-
ed Service Award in
1989. He is buried in
the Tuskegee Univer-
sity cemetery.

EPHRAIM M. HENRY'S TUSKEGEE
DIPLOMA WITH ITS ORIGINAL COVER.

Ephraim M. Henry graduated from the
Tuskegee Institute with a Bachelor of Science
in Education degree on May 24, 1934.

RADIO
CITY
MUSIC
HALL

FIFTIETH STREET
AND SIXTH AVE.
NEW YORK

TWO PERFORMANCES
DAILY..2.15..8.15 P. M.

BEGINNING
DECEMBER 27, 1932

PHOTOGRAPHIC ALBUM RELATING
TO THE LINCOLN NORMAL SCHOOL
IN MARION, ALABAMA.

The Lincoln Normal School was
chartered in 1867, due to the efforts of
the American Missionary Association
(AMA) and the Freedman's Bureau.
The site was selected by the AMA,
which began working with local
former slaves to raise capital for the
project. The AMA leased a building
in 1868 and the following year began raising
funds for a building of its own. Appropria-
tions by the Alabama state legislature in 1870
and 1871 led to the state approving the establishment of four teacher-training facilities,
and in 1873 the AMA deeded the school to
the state with the understanding that it
would be used as a normal college for
African American students.

The school was split in 1887, and
the training of teachers was moved to a site
in Montgomery, which even-
tually became Alabama State
University. The facility in Marion
burned to the ground that year
under questionable circumstances.
The school underwent incredible
hardships to reopen and remain
viable. Under the guidance of Mary
Elizabeth Phillips, principal from
1896 until her death in 1927, the
school prospered. With the ending
of segregation the AMA, which had
continued to subsidize the school,
severed its connection, and from that time
forward the school was operated by the state.
The school ceased operation in 1970, but its
legacy among African American students in
Alabama will be long remembered.

PHOTOS RIGHT, TOP TO BOTTOM:
*"Normal practice room, student
teacher in the rear"; Page from the
album; "After the birthday party—
Mrs. Herchmer, teacher"; "Next! No
waiting! Lincoln Normal kindergarten";
"New Building—built 1922 Lincoln
Normal School 'Hartford Room' Here."*

Original cover of the Lincoln Normal School photograph album.

PHOTOGRAPH OF EMPLOYEES OF THE
AFRICAN AMERICAN–OWNED ATLANTA
LIFE INSURANCE COMPANY TAKEN IN
MACON, GEORGIA, BY THE WOODALL
STUDIO.

Alonzo Franklin Herndon (1858–1927) was born into slavery in Walton County, Georgia. While Herndon was growing up in Social Circle, Georgia, his family were sharecroppers, and young Herndon worked variously as a laborer and a peddler. In 1878 he left Social Circle and eventually learned the barbering trade, establishing a barber shop in Jonesboro, Georgia. Moving to Atlanta in 1883, he was quite successful and by 1904 owned three barber shops with a regional reputation. Herndon invested in Atlanta real estate and in 1905 purchased the Atlanta Mutual Insurance Association. He reorganized that concern in 1922 as the Atlanta Life Insurance Company. Herndon was a community leader and philanthropist, giving his support to the YMCA, Atlanta University, several orphanages, and numerous other institutions.

The 1923 diploma awarded to John Washington Dickinson for completing the Atlanta Life Insurance Company's salesmanship course. The diploma is signed by Alonzo F. Herndon, the company's founder and president.

PSYCHO BEAUTIGRAPH ETCHING OF
GEORGE WASHINGTON CARVER FROM
1946 BY FELIX B. GAINES.

George Washington Carver (1864–1943) was born into slavery in Missouri and was orphaned at an early age. George and his brother James were then raised by the white Carver family. Carver received some home schooling but traveled to other parts of Missouri to further his education, finally graduating from high school in Kansas.

Carver tried his hand at homesteading in Kansas and established a farm near Beeler, where he also pursued a youthful interest in botany. Attending Simpson College in Iowa, he excelled at music and art, but a teacher, recognizing his keen interest in agriculture, urged him to tranfer to the Iowa State Agricultural College in Ames. He became the first black student to attend the school and the first African American faculty member. His work in plant pathology and mycology there gained him a national reputation.

Booker T. Washington invited Carver to head the Agriculture Department at the Tuskegee Institute in 1896. Carver would remain there for forty-seven years, building a nationally recognized program at the institute and continuing his research into new uses for peanuts, sweet potatoes, soybeans, and other crops. His contributions to agricultural progress in the South and the nation mark him as one of the greatest of American scientists.

RIGHT: *PRODUCTS BY DR. CARVER* (1952) BY FELIX B. GAINES.

Overlayed on a stylized map of Alabama are 300 products developed by Carver and 175 byproducts. Included is a quote by Carver: "I work under the direction of God."

PAGES FROM A 1943 PROGRAM FOR A THANKSGIVING DINNER SERVED AT THE TUSKEGEE ARMY AIR FIELD.

The menu offered young roast turkey, baked Virginia ham, candied sweet potatoes, pumpkin pie, and ice cream.

Tuskegee Army Air Field was home to the highly decorated 332nd Fighter Group, the Tuskegee Airmen, commanded by Colonel Benjamin O. Davis Jr. Davis went on to be the first African American general in the US Air Force.

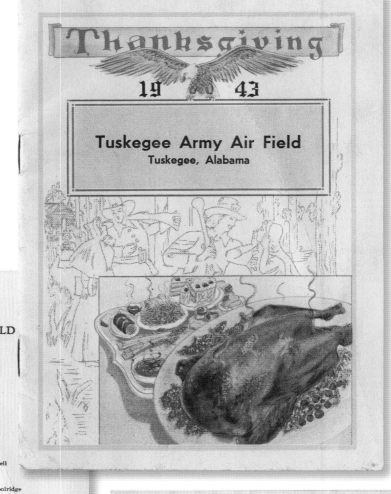

TUSKEGEE ARMY AIR FIELD
TUSKEGEE, ALABAMA

Colonel Noel F. Parrish
COMMANDING

★

BASE MESS OFFICER
Lt. Douglas Jones

GENERAL MESS NUMBER ONE

OFFICER PERSONNEL

Lt. William J. Silvers, Jr.   Lt. Vincent O. Campbell

ENLISTED PERSONNEL

S/Sgt. Carl W. Warren	S/Sgt. Walter W. Woolridge
Sgt. Herbert T. McAllister	Sgt. Charles D. Leath
Cpl. Robert W. Saunders	Cpl. Ralph C. Warren
Cpl. Robert L. Glover	Cpl. Sherman J. Matthews
Pfc. Henry McMillan	Pfc. Thomas C. Styles
Pfc. William H. Anderson	Pfc. Gennie Laws
Pfc. James Collins	Pvt. Alexander Edwards
Pvt. Edward Alexander	Pvt. James Bennett

ORGANIZATIONS

318th Base Hq. & A. B. Sq.

Captain Bascom F. Hodge   Lt. Bayard K. Colon
Lt. Winston Sims   Lt. William L. Roberts, Jr.

318th Air Base Detachment

Lt. Julian S. Peasant, Jr.   Lt. Mannie M. Watkins
Lt. Henry Moses

1451st Quartermaster Company Aviation (Serv)

Lt. Fred P. Wright   Lt. Isaac A. Groom

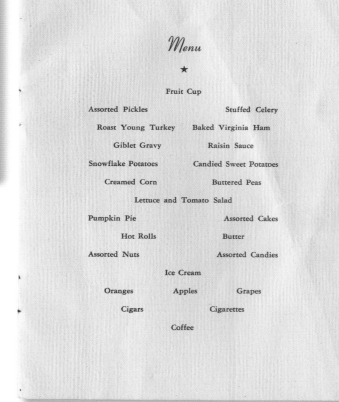

Menu
★

Fruit Cup

Assorted Pickles	Stuffed Celery
Roast Young Turkey	Baked Virginia Ham
Giblet Gravy	Raisin Sauce
Snowflake Potatoes	Candied Sweet Potatoes
Creamed Corn	Buttered Peas

Lettuce and Tomato Salad

Pumpkin Pie	Assorted Cakes
Hot Rolls	Butter
Assorted Nuts	Assorted Candies

Ice Cream

Oranges   Apples   Grapes

Cigars   Cigarettes

Coffee

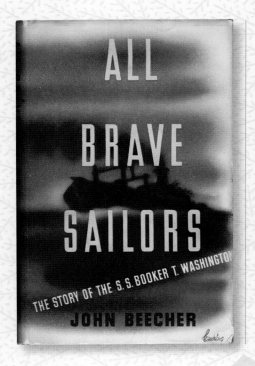

Front cover of John Beecher's *All Brave Sailors: The Story of the S.S. "Booker T. Washington"* (New York: L. B. Fischer, 1945). A nonfiction account of the Merchant Marine service of the S.S. *Booker T. Washington*.

The ship, commissioned in 1942, was the first in the Merchant Marine commanded by an African American. It also carried the first integrated crew to serve under an African American captain.

John Beecher (1904–1980), the white author, served on the *Washington* as purser. *All Brave Sailors* was Beecher's first book. A noted Alabama poet, he was the great-grandnephew of Harriet Beecher Stowe.

Though Beecher was born in New York City, his family moved to Birmingham, Alabama, in 1907 where his father was a steel-industry executive.

After being injured in a steel mill accident in 1925, Beecher began his educational career in earnest, attending both Harvard University and the University of North Carolina, where he worked under Howard W. Odum. His experiences in the steel mills and during the Great Depression led to his labor and civil rights activism. His books of poetry express his belief in social justice and equality.

Signed first edition copy of Martin Luther King Jr.'s *Strength to Love* (New York: Harper and Row, 1963).

The Williams Collection copy of *Strength to Love* is signed on the free endpaper.

IX.
ART OF THE SOUTH IN BLACK AND WHITE: EDWIN HARLESTON, HOWARD WEEDEN, AND ALLEN REDWOOD

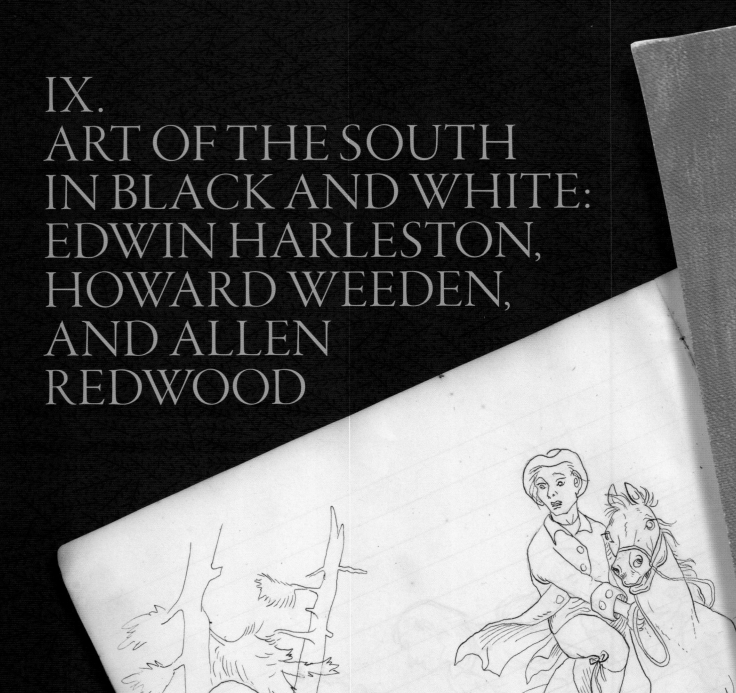

Works by
Edwin Harleston
and Howard Weeden.
   The Williams Collection
includes works by two important southern artists: oil portaits
and figure studies by Edwin Harleston, and a Howard Weeden notebook with drawings illustrating "The
Legend of Sleepy Hollow."

T he A. S. Williams III Americana Collection contains notable items by three important southern artists.

Edwin Augustus Harleston (1882–1931), a native of Charleston, South Carolina, was one of the most distinguished artists and civil rights leaders of his generation, founding the Charleston branch of the NAACP in 1916. Primarily a portraitist, he painted a number of prominent Americans both black and white during his career. The Williams Collection holds a number of untitled portraits, as well as some anatomical drawings, from this noted African American artist.

Maria Howard Weeden (1846–1905) was a native of Huntsville, Alabama. An accomplished artist and author, she wrote and illustrated four books. She is represented in the collection by several watercolors and some wonderful pen and ink illustrations depicting scenes from Washington Irving's "The Legend of Sleepy Hollow." Many of her notable works are depictions of African American personalities.

Allen Carter Redwood (1844–1922), Confederate soldier and artist, was born in Lancaster County, Virginia. After the Civil War he became a well-known artist and illustrator, primarily through his connection with the *Century* magazine and their well-known series *Battles and Leaders of the Civil War*. Redwood also wrote of his Confederate service in several articles related to the common soldier.

MARIA HOWARD WEEDEN. *THE BANKS OF THE TENNESSEE RIVER, NEAR HUNTSVILLE*. WATERCOLOR, 11 x 19.24 INCHES.

Maria Howard Weeden (1846–1905), the renowned portraitist and author, was born in Huntsville, Alabama. Weeden's father, William Donaldson Weeden, died six months before her birth. She was educated at the Huntsville Female Seminary, where she showed an early talent in art and music. Her mother, Jane Urquhart Weeden, arranged for her to have private art lessons.

Refugees after the Union occupation of Huntsville during the Civil War, Weeden, her mother, and her sister Kate moved to a plantation near Tuskegee owned by an older daughter. The end of the war found the Weeden family impoverished, and to assist the family Maria taught art classes and began selling her artwork.

Weeden became interested in poetry written in black dialect, and inspired by Sarah Pratt McLean Greene's "De Massa ob de Sheepfol," she produced a hand-bound book from it, which she illustrated. The cover was a remarkable illustration of a local freedman. Due to her myopia and the fact that she used a brush with only three hairs, the detail astonished many who saw it.

After a trip to Chicago for the World's Columbian Exposition in 1893, Weeden came to realize that much of the art depicting former slaves and free persons of African American heritage was based on

stereotypical caricatures. From this she began to paint Huntsville blacks with whom she had personal ties and later sought out other subjects, usually former slaves of friends and neighbors.

Weeden's interest in African American dialect poetry resulted in her writing, illustrating, and binding one-of-a-kind books in this genre. Some of her paintings were shown in exhibits in Berlin and Paris through the influence of her friend Elizabeth Price, which brought Weeden international notice.

After a local resident saw some of her poetry and illustrations, he consulted a small publisher in Boston about their possibilities, and the result was Weeden's first book *Shadows on the Wall* (1898). She wrote

three other books, *Bandanna Ballads* (1899), *Songs of the Old South* (1901), and *Old Voices* (1904). Through these volumes, she achieved her goal of painting the African Americans of her acquaintance with love and respect as well as recording the stories and personalities of those remarkable people.

Original cover and title page of Maria Howard
Weeden's notebook containing sketches for
"The Legend of Sleepy Hollow."

ABOVE: MARIA HOWARD WEEDEN'S ORIGINAL SKETCHES FOR
"THE LEGEND OF SLEEPY HOLLOW."

ALLEN CARTER REDWOOD, *TALKING TO THE ORDERLY*, WATERCOLOR, SIGNED A.C.R., 1883.

Talking to the Orderly was originally titled *Instructions to the Orderly* and was engraved to accompany an article in the *St. Nicholas* magazine for October of 1883.

Allen Carter Redwood (1844–1922) was born in Lancaster County, Virginia. Redwood's middle name is sometimes given as Christian, but his mother was a Carter before her marriage.

He was educated privately in Baltimore and at the Polytechnic Institute of Brooklyn, New York. At the outbreak of the war he returned to Virginia and joined the Confederate army. He first served in a Maryland cavalry unit, but he later transferred to the Fifty-fifth Virginia Infantry. During the course of the war Redwood was wounded three times and captured twice. He is one of a small number of Civil War artists who actually served in the military.

After the war he moved to Baltimore then to New York to pursue his artistic career. He worked for both the Harper Publishing Company and the *Century* magazine. His association with the *Century* resulted in both numerous illustrations and a written article for their famous series *Battles and Leaders of the Civil War*. Redwood also contributed an article "The Confederate in the Field" for the ten-volume *Photographic History of the Civil War*. Redwood spent some time in the West, drawing primarily US cavalry units, and made some sketches relating to the Spanish-American War. His most famous Western illustration is *The Card Game*, an oil painting done in 1895. It depicts the disputed outcome of one of the perennial games of chance.

four years later received a BA from Atlanta University. Edwin studied for a period at the School of the Museum of Fine Arts in Boston, returning to Charleston in 1913 to assist his father in the operation of the family funeral home. When a chapter of the NAACP was founded in Charleston in 1916, he was elected its first president.

Harleston married Elise Forrest (1891–1970), a photographer, in 1920, after the two had opened an art and photograph studio in Charleston. Harleston's spare time from that business and the funeral home was spent in furthering his art education and securing commissions. He studied at the Art Institute of Chicago in the summer of 1925 and that year was commissioned to paint the portrait of philanthropist Pierre Samuel DuPont. His last important work was assisting African American artist Aaron Douglas (1899–1979) in painting the well-known murals at Fisk University in Nashville. Harleston also painted Douglas's portrait at that time. Prior to Harleston's death he was awarded the Harmon Foundation's prestiguous Alain Locke prize for portraiture.

CHARCOAL SELF-PORTRAIT OF EDWIN HARLESTON.

Edwin Augustus "Teddy" Harleston (1882–1931) was the grandson of William Harleston (1804–1874), a white plantation owner in Charleston, South Carolina. Harleston never married but had eight children by Kate Wilson (1825–1886), an African American and his former slave, one whom was Edwin Gaillard Harleston, the artist's father.

Edwin Harleston was valedictorian at the Avery Institute in Charleston in 1900 and

FACING PAGE: EDWIN HARLESTON, UNIDENTIED PORTRAIT, OIL ON CANVAS.

Edwin Harleston, unidentied portraits, oil on canvas.

EDWIN HARLESTON, NUDE STUDIES,
OIL ON CANVAS.

X.
STRAIGHT TO THE SOURCE: MANUSCRIPTS AND SPECIAL ARCHIVES

ORIGINAL BINDING FOR GUEST REGISTER OF MOBILE'S FAMOUS BATTLE HOUSE HOTEL.

This register from mid-1863 includes notable guests such as Confedrate generals Joseph E. Johnston and John C. Breck-inridge; Captain A. H. Keller, father of Helen Keller; Horace L. Hunley, inventor of the first submarine to sink an enemy ship; Henry Wirz, commandant of the infamous Confederate prison at Andersonville, Georgia; notorious Confederate spy Belle Boyd; John A. Campbell, Alabama's first US Supreme Court justice; and Mobile novelist Augusta Evans.

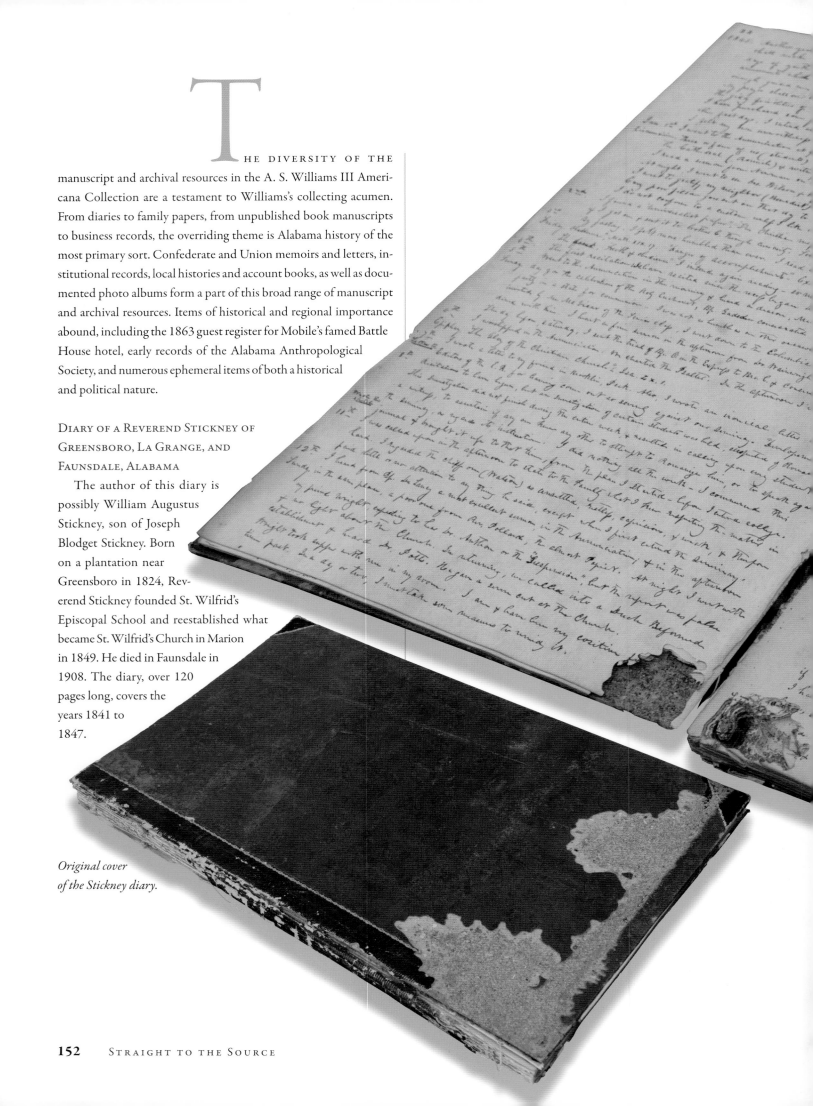

T HE DIVERSITY OF THE
manuscript and archival resources in the A. S. Williams III Americana Collection are a testament to Williams's collecting acumen.
From diaries to family papers, from unpublished book manuscripts
to business records, the overriding theme is Alabama history of the
most primary sort. Confederate and Union memoirs and letters, institutional records, local histories and account books, as well as documented photo albums form a part of this broad range of manuscript
and archival resources. Items of historical and regional importance
abound, including the 1863 guest register for Mobile's famed Battle
House hotel, early records of the Alabama Anthropological
Society, and numerous ephemeral items of both a historical
and political nature.

DIARY OF A REVEREND STICKNEY OF GREENSBORO, LA GRANGE, AND FAUNSDALE, ALABAMA

The author of this diary is
possibly William Augustus
Stickney, son of Joseph
Blodget Stickney. Born
on a plantation near
Greensboro in 1824, Rev-
erend Stickney founded St. Wilfrid's
Episcopal School and reestablished what
became St. Wilfrid's Church in Marion
in 1849. He died in Faunsdale in
1908. The diary, over 120
pages long, covers the
years 1841 to
1847.

*Original cover
of the Stickney diary.*

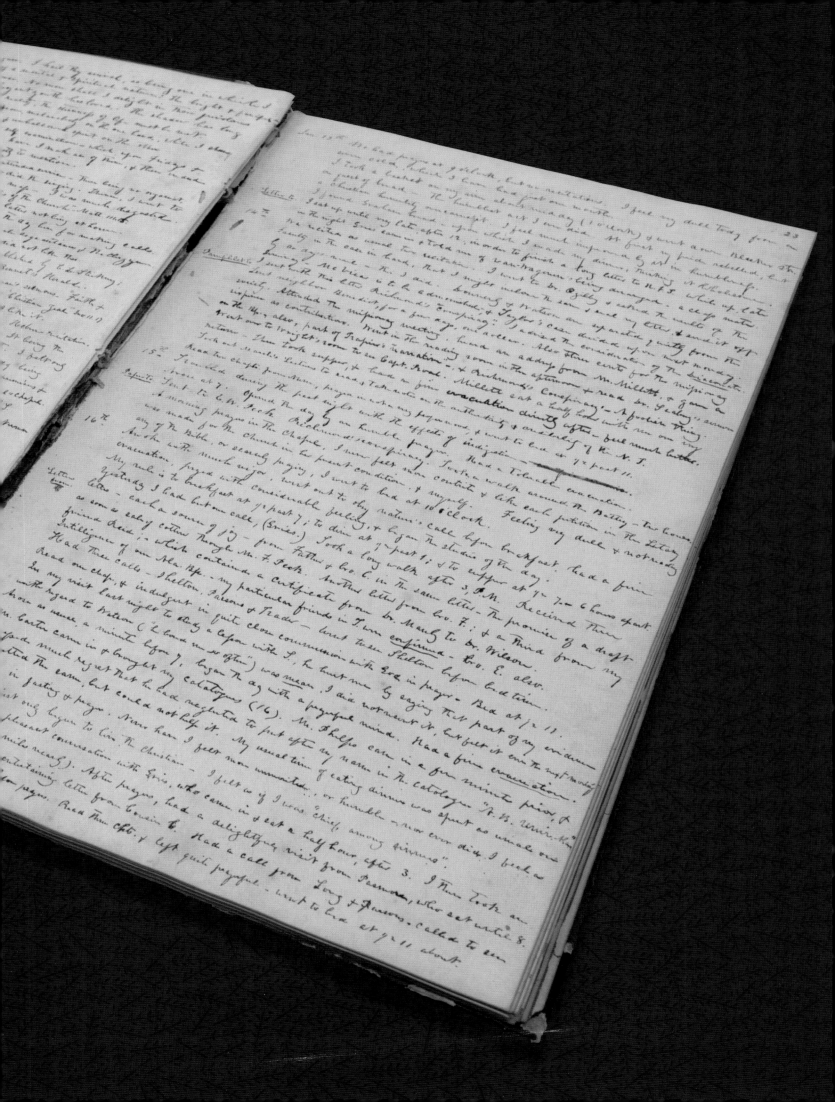

The Williams Collection includes both manuscripts and printed sources related to the Union side of the Civil War. The letters of George Woodward, a soldier in the Eighth Wisconsin, form part of this extensive collection.

George Woodward enlisted in the fall of 1861 and was sent to Camp Randall, near Madison, Wisconsin. He began a correspondence with his fiancée, Gene Smith of Dodge County, Wisconsin, that lasted from October 1861 through November 1863.

By happenstance, there was another man with virtually the same name in the regiment, a Sergeant George T. Woodward of Company D. This unfortunate soldier succumbed to chronic diarrhea in the hospital at Memphis, Tennessee, on January 31, 1863. This letter intended for his wife was misdirected to Gene Smith in one of those odd occurrences that sometimes happen in war.

LEFT: ORIGINAL COPY OF GEORGE W. DRIGGS'S REGIMENTAL HISTORY *OPENING OF THE MISSISSIPPI; OR TWO YEARS CAMPAIGNING IN THE SOUTHWEST. A RECORD OF THE CAMPAIGNS, SIEGES, ACTIONS AND MARCHES IN WHICH THE 8TH WISCONSIN VOLUNTEERS HAVE PARTICIPATED* (MADISON, WI: WM. J. PARK & CO., 1864).

E. Merton Coulter's Civil War bibliography calls this "a remarkably interesting and valuable commentary on the country and its people. The writing is somewhat humorous and 'smart,' but there is little bias or bitterness."

N. Town Heaton

Corinth Miss
June 1st 1862

Jack!

The great Battle of Corinth, was passed and
we now occupy the place. This great battle was
fought & the victory won with but little loss on
our part, one of the 91st received a wound in the
thigh. on the 28th the whole army advanced to
attact the forces at that place, our Division in
the right wing Buel in the centre Pope on
the left all being Supported by a large reserve. our
Regt & Brigad was in the advance. we marched out
of our breast works and advanced about a quarter of a
mile where we came to the reble pickets, they fired
on our Skirmishers but they made no halt drove
them back about half a mile where they Seemed to
have concentrated quite a force and was in line
of battle. here the Battery that was in our Brigade
commenced pouring in Shell grape & canister
this cleared them from this place. orders now came to
halt for the night. all laying on their arms, just

could be heard along the lines, into them they
went almost double quick. within their
breastworks: we now began to see tents & cots, blankets
camp kettles and every thing pertaining to an army.

Secesh he came to much that the officer arrested
her this cooled her off quite suddenly

Yours
T. Heaton M.D.

ORIGINAL MANUSCRIPT LETTER FROM
DR. TOWNE HEATON OF OHIO.

This letter, part of an extensive archive
related to Heaton, was written on June 1,
1862, to his brother John (Jack) Heaton in
Fincastle, Ohio, and describes the Battle of
Corinth, Mississippi.

Towne Heaton enlisted in the
Seventieth Ohio Infantry at Ben-
tonville, Ohio, in October 1861 and
served primarily in the capacity of
regimental surgeon. Prior to his discharge in December 1864 he wrote the
thirty letters that comprise
this archive to his brother.

The letter from Corinth
states that the Confederate
army was greatly demoral-
ized and that "it is thought
that many of them would
make their way home and cease
to fight for 'Jeff the
Great.'" Upon enter-
ing Corinth, Heaton's
regiment encountered
some citizens claiming
to be Unionists, but "we
found one young lady that
was strong Secesh . . . so
much that the officer arrested
her, this cooled her off quite
suddenly."

A letter from Holly Springs,
Mississippi, in December 1862
gives a good description of the
Confederate raid on that Federal
base. Two letters were written from
Alabama, one from Bridgeport in December 1863 and one from Scottsboro
the following month.

GUEST REGISTER OF MOBILE'S FAMOUS BATTLE HOUSE HOTEL.

This register covers the period from March 1 to September 26, 1863. A preliminary inventory of Confederate notables and others accompanies the register.

RIGHT: CLOSE UP OF THE BATTLE HOUSE HOTEL GUEST REGISTER SHOWING THE SIGNATURE OF CAPTAIN ARTHUR HENLEY KELLER OF THE TWENTY-SEVENTH ALABAMA REGIMENT.

Keller (1836–1896) was a native of Tuscumbia and studied law at the University of Virginia before the Civil War. He returned to his law practice after the war until 1874 when he purchased the *Tuscumbia North Alabamian* newspaper. Keller edited this newspaper until his death. In 1878 he married his second wife, Kate Adams, and in 1880 they had their first child, Alabama's renowned Helen Adams Keller.

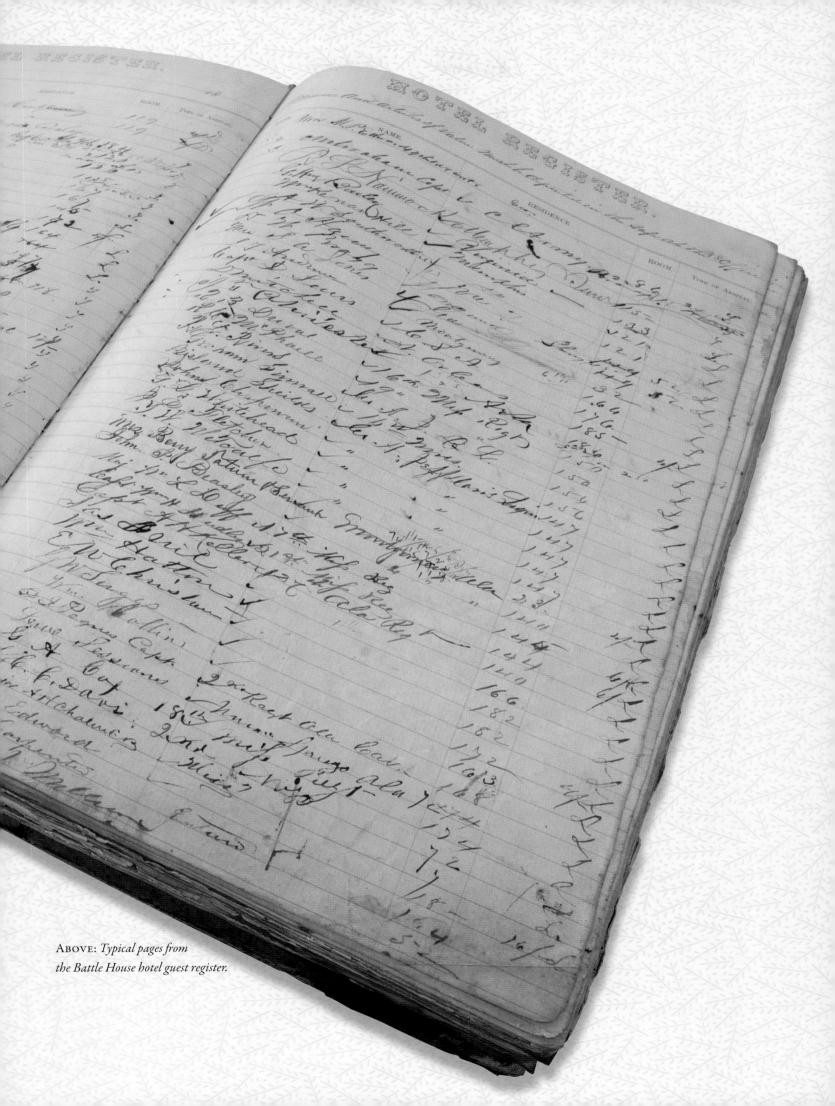

ABOVE: *Typical pages from the Battle House hotel guest register.*

An 1883 sketchbook of drawings made by Sergeant F. Zelinski of the First Regiment Infantry, Alabama State Troops at Camp O'Neal, Frascati, Alabama. Zelinski presented the sketchbook to C. L. Tyler of Mobile.

Frascati Park was located on the western part of Mobile Bay and was founded in 1867 by Henry Nabring, owner of the Battle House hotel. The park was later purchased by Martin Horst, who developed it as a getaway spot for well-to-do citizens of Mobile. The park had a hotel and a restaurant as well as facilities for staging operas and open-air concerts. Oscar Wilde gave a lecture at Frascati in 1882. It was a popular spot for social gatherings and picnics. Annual encampments of the Alabama National Guard were held there. Frascati was located at the end of Old Shell Road and was virtually demolished by a severe hurricane in 1893.

BELOW: Escorting Governor O'Neal into Camp *from Zelinski's sketchbook.*

Escorting Governor O'Neal into Camp.

The evening gun.

JUNE

CAMP

1st REGT. INF.

AT

FRASCATI.

BELLUM. SI. VIS. PACEM. PARA

'NEAL.

ALA. ST. TR.

1883.

MINUTES OF THE MONTGOMERY CITY
INFIRMARY BOARD OF PHYSICIANS AND
SURGEONS.

Ledger style book containing the manuscript minutes of the Montgomery City Infirmary Board of Physicians and Surgeons from 1888 to 1896. The minutes cover twenty-three pages.

RIGHT: *Minutes of the first meeting of the Montgomery City Infirmary Board of Physicians and Surgeons, held on March 24, 1888, in the hall of the Medical and Surgical Society of Montgomery County in the City Building at the corner of Munroe and Perry Streets.*

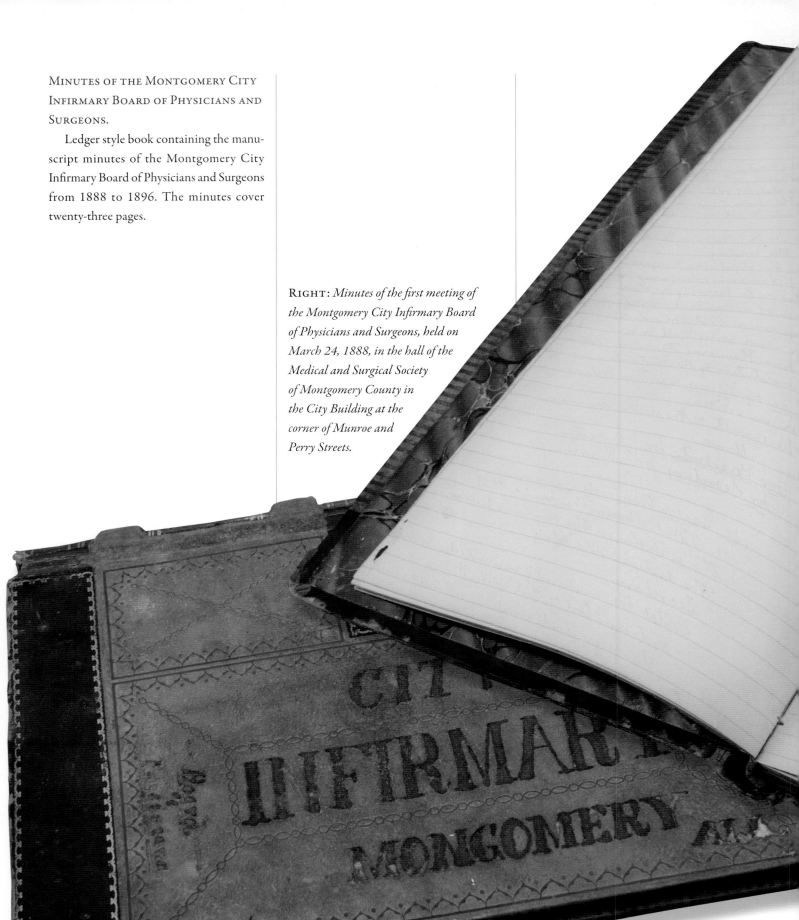

ABOVE: *Original binding of the minutes of the Montgomery City Infirmary Board of Physicians and Surgeons.*

Montgomery City Infirmary

The first meeting of the Board of Physicians and Surgeons of the Montgomery City Infirmary took place in the Hall of the Montgomery County Medical & Surgical Society of Montgomery corner Monroe & Perry streets on March 24th 1888. The following minutes show the business transacted at that meeting.

Hall Med & Surg Society Ala '88
March 24th

On motion of Dr. R.F. Michel, Dr. W.C. Jackson was called to the chair. Dr. J.R. Jordan was requested to act as secretary.

Dr. Jackson asked Dr. B.J. Baldwin to state the object of the meeting.

Dr. Baldwin said the object was to organize the Board of Physicians & Surgeons (which had been elected by the Board of Trustees) by the election of a President & Secretary.

Dr. J.D. Selby moved that the article, which we were going to act, be read.

Dr. Baldwin then read the article under the constitution of the Institution.

The election of Officers was then declared to be in order.

The result of the election was as follows:

For President: Dr. J.B. Gaston.
For Secretary: Dr. J.R. Jordan.

Officers for 1888.

Dr. Gaston then took the chair. Dr. W.M. Wilkerson then moved that the articles in the By Laws, prescribing the duties of the Staff, be read by the Secretary.

After the reading of said articles, Dr. Selby criticised Art. 7. that "at least two of the consultants should be notified & should

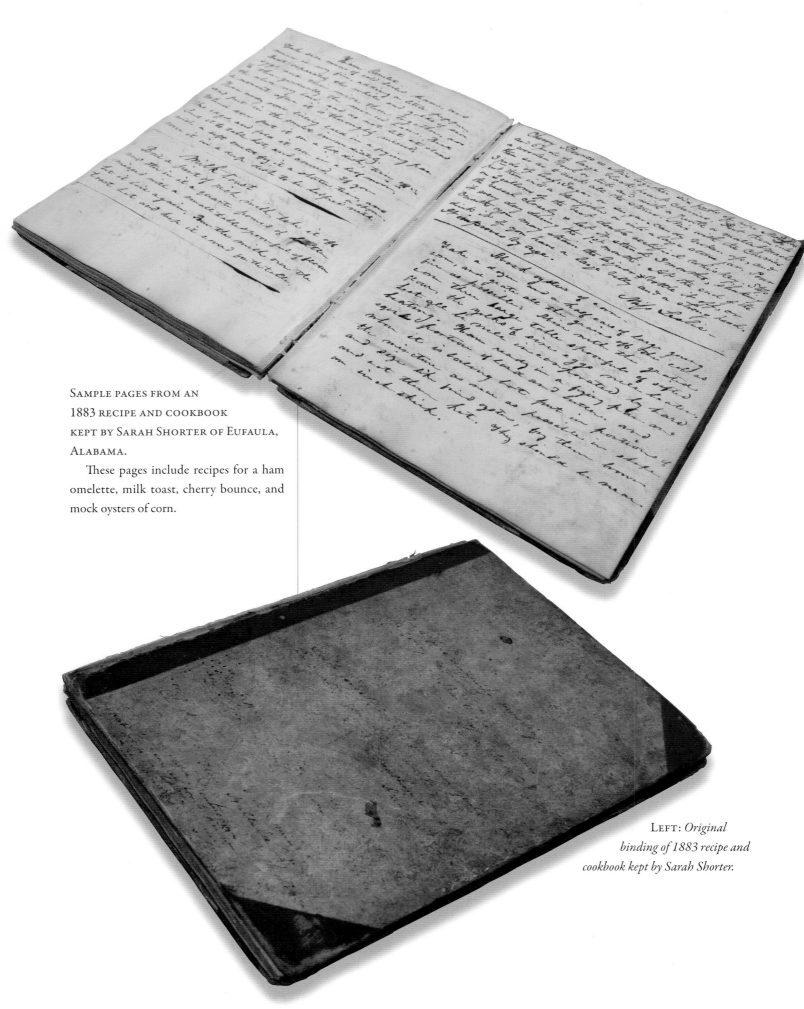

Sample pages from an 1883 recipe and cookbook kept by Sarah Shorter of Eufaula, Alabama.

These pages include recipes for a ham omelette, milk toast, cherry bounce, and mock oysters of corn.

Left: *Original binding of 1883 recipe and cookbook kept by Sarah Shorter.*

Typescripts and correspondence file relating to sisters Alice and Margaret Alison, two of Alabama's most prolific authors.

Two of the most fascinating (and least publicized) of Alabama's female authors were two sisters, Margaret and Alice Alison of Richmond, Alabama. Daughters of Joseph D. and Annie Hearst Alison, the girls were raised in a very traditional southern manner. Both attended Converse College in South Carolina as well as Columbia University in New York. Margaret spent a year at the University of Alabama in between.

Margaret (1896–1959) wrote a prize story while in college, prompting a friendly competition with her older sister Alice (1890–1955). Alice published her first book, *Inemak: The Little Greenlander,* in 1927 with Rand-McNally. The two collaborated on *Ood-Le-Uk* *the Wanderer* in 1930. Published by Little, Brown, it became a Literary Guild selection. Under the pseudonym Hugh McAllister they published four books together before 1930.

The sisters chose husbands whose personal interests influenced their writings. Alice married Tom Lide, who had a personal interest in people of the far north, which led to *Inemak.* Margaret married Carl Johansen, a native of Denmark, and the flavor of Scandinavia runs through a number of their books. The two wrote over ten books together and over five singly. Alice also coauthored a book with her mother, entitled *Tambalo and Other Stories of Far Lands,* published in 1930.

Their correspondence and a number of typescripts of published manuscripts are in the Williams Collection. One of the typescripts is a possibly unpublished juvenile life of Booker T. Washington.

Pages from *1920 Photos and Clippings, Alabama Anthropological Society, Photos by Tresslar, Burnham and Brannon,* an album relating to field trips by the Alabama Anthropological Society.

The society was founded in 1909 by Thomas M. Owen, Peter A. Brannon, and Henry S. Halbert. Owen was at that time director of the Alabama Department of Archives and History. This group was not made up of professional archaeologists, but individuals who shared a serious interest in the anthropology of the state. The society held meetings and performed a number of excavations on early Native American sites.

In 1920 Peter Brannon, the group's secretary, was primarily responsible for founding *Arrow Points,* a journal documenting the society's activities.

The 1930s witnessed the beginnings of other, professionally staffed programs in this area. Owen died in 1920, and Brannon had been given the job of curator of the Department of Archives and History under the new director, Marie Bankhead Owen, the widow of the former director.

The publication of *Arrow Points* ceased in 1937 and with it the formal existence of the society. The Alabama Department of Archives and History is the depository of many of the group's excavated artifacts.

Two political badges from a collection formed by Peter A. Brannon

Brannon's collection also included commemorative badges, campaign buttons, and materials related to reunions of Confederate fraternal and memorial associations.

Oscar W. Underwood (1862–1929) served Alabama in both the US House of Representatives and Senate (1915–1927), and is the only individual to have served as Democratic leader in both houses. Underwood made strong bids for the Democratic presidential nomination in 1912 and 1924. His strong opposition to prohibition and the Ku Klux Klan spelled the end of his political career.

On the way to Perry Co, June 10.

Writing for Holt
near Mulberry

Water Hyacinths
in mill pond 12 miles
above Selma.

Fish pond.

Near Spratt.

Graft at the well.

On the way to Perry Co, June 10

Burnham's car

P.O. at Felix

Seated, left to right,
top row:
    Baldi
    Oswalt
    Thompson
    Holt, J.
    Matthews (guest)
    Paterson
2nd row:
    Bird (guest)
    Brumm, W.
    Lewes, C.R.
    — anson, M.D.

At Y. Building at Ecunhutke
May 28 —
photo by Burnham

Standing:
    Tumble
    Spangler (guest)
    Presslar, M. (guest)
    Edwards
Kneeling, near —
    Bild
    Juniors:
    Spangler
    Pitts
    Brunion
    Paterson
    Marks

INDEX

ABOUT THE AUTHOR

Stephen M. Rowe is archivist and curator of the Eufaula Athenaeum, Eufaula, Alabama. A native of Richmond, Virginia, and a graduate of North Carolina State University at Raleigh, he was an assistant archivist at the Colonial Williamsburg Foundation from 1974 to 1977. Since 1983 he has worked as an antiquarian bookseller and appraiser.